COMING OUT

COMING OUT

The New Dynamics

Nicholas A. Guittar

FIRST**FORUM**PRESS

A DIVISION OF LYNNE RIENNER PUBLISHERS, INC. • BOULDER & LONDON

Published in the United States of America in 2014 by
FirstForumPress
A division of Lynne Rienner Publishers, Inc.
1800 30th Street, Boulder, Colorado 80301
www.firstforumpress.com

and in the United Kingdom by
FirstForumPress
A division of Lynne Rienner Publishers, Inc.
3 Henrietta Street, Covent Garden, London WC2E 8LU

Library of Congress Cataloging-in-Publication Data
Guittar, Nicholas A.
Coming out: the new dynamics / Nicholas A. Guittar.
Includes bibliographical references and index.
ISBN 978-1-62637-043-2 (hc: alk. paper)
1. Coming out (Sexual orientation) 2. Gays—Identity. 3. Sexual orientation. I. Title.
HQ76.25.G85 2014
306.76'6—dc23   2013049826

British Cataloguing in Publication Data
A Cataloguing in Publication record for this book
is available from the British Library.

This book was produced from digital files prepared by the author
using the FirstForumComposer.

Printed and bound in the United States of America

∞   The paper used in this publication meets the requirements
     of the American National Standard for Permanence of
     Paper for Printed Library Materials Z39.48-1992.

5 4 3 2 1

Contents

Acknowledgments

This project is very much a labor of love. The book is dedicated to those whose voices are not heard and to anyone whose sexual identity has been ignored, challenged, or trivialized. The success of this project owes heavily to the participants in the study, each of whom provided me with such rich and engaging coming out experiences—your narratives inspire me every day, and I wish you all the best in your future endeavors.

I owe a great many thanks to the people who provided me with the tools necessary to engage in this research. I am particularly indebted to Liz Grauerholz—my mentor, collaborator, and friend—for her advice, expertise, and encouragement. Although I was helped by so many other people, I would particularly like to thank Betsy Lucal, Shannon Carter, John Lynxwiler, Fernando Rivera, Rachel Rayburn, and Jim Wright. Your input and expertise strengthened the project throughout. I would like to collectively thank the Department of Sociology at the University of Central Florida for the opportunity to develop as a scholar—go Knights! Special thanks go also to Andrew Berzanskis, acquisitions editor at Lynne Rienner Publishers, for believing in this work and providing me with the platform to reach a broader audience. I would like to recognize my amazing parents, Mary and Ronald Guittar, for being such outstanding role models and the providers of constant encouragement and support.

Last, but certainly not least, I must graciously thank my partner and in-house colleague, Stephanie Gonzalez Guittar. Few people enjoy the privilege of having a partner who shares their passions in life, and for this I am forever grateful. It began with intrigue and it continues with love and admiration . . .

1

The Shifting Contexts of Coming Out

When I was little all I could think about was me under a fucking hopa [a Jewish altar], getting married and the guy stepping on the fucking glass, and having an awesome crazy-big wedding because I'm very big like that, and that's all I could think about . . . you think about your wedding day as a little girl. And, playing Barbie . . . Barbie and Ken, you make them fuck, you don't make the two . . . well, maybe you do make the two girls fuck, but you know what I mean. That's always how it's been and the all of the sudden you either meet people who are like this, or you are just realizing or you find that you have this attraction toward this person or that person, and you just don't understand why and it's something that's deep inside of you.

~Gabrielle

Gabrielle has plenty of reasons to demonstrate a heightened sense of frustration—perhaps even anger—and it all comes through in this single quote. Within this dialog we see very clearly the normative expectation of "man + woman" (i.e., heteronormativity), and we see that it operates on so many levels. Heteronormativity lives in our institutions, it permeates our culture, and it governs much of our social interaction. Like so many of the participants in this study, Gabrielle spoke about the powerful influences of heteronormativity on her sexuality and her life as a whole. Social forces rooted in normative sexual arrangements shackled her to heterosexuality throughout childhood and adolescence, even as she began to recognize having feelings toward members of the same sex. As time progressed Gabrielle became increasingly aware of the fact that her sexuality would add additional challenges to many facets of life. Participants in the current study spoke frequently of various heteronormative expectations placed upon them by their parents, themselves, and society at large (e.g., to date members of the other sex, get married, etc.).

Heterosexuality is still the norm in contemporary life throughout the United States (Katz 2007). Lesbian, gay, bisexual, and queer (LGBQ) individuals, all of whom have a sexual orientation that falls outside of this dominant heterosexual framework, face myriad difficulties associated with identifying and maintaining healthy sexual identities (Rust 1993). Central to these challenges is "coming out," which has been identified as one of the most crucial elements in the development of a healthy sexual identity (McLean 2007).

Some contemporary scholars suggest that coming out is no longer a relevant concept related to the formation and maintenance of sexual identities. Although the concept of "coming out" is undergoing massive transformation, it continues to impact people's lives in meaningful ways. At the heart of this study are the experiences of 30 people who collectively demonstrate how heteronormativity continues to assert its influence over all "other" sexualities. For starters, "coming out" does not have a singular, shared meaning—as so many scholars purport. Coming out is not even necessarily about the outward disclosure of one's sexual identity. For some people, coming out is entirely a matter of accepting and affirming their own sexuality (i.e., coming out to oneself). Quite simply, the meanings of coming out are as varied as the individuals who engage in such a career.

An extensive body of literature exists with regard to why an individual may choose *not* to come out. However, this research project illuminates an equally important interaction—how social forces influence the way in which an individual *does* come out. For example, many participants in the current study engaged in an interaction I call the *queer apologetic*—coming out initially as bisexual despite being interested *only* in members of the same sex. The queer apologetic is essentially an identity compromise based in the rationale that bisexuality simultaneously satisfies 1) their personal attractions to only members of the same sex, and 2) society's expectation that they be attracted to members of the other sex. The queer apologetic is just one example of how coming out is still quite relevant—even at a time when increasingly fewer people remain "closeted." In addition to the queer apologetic there are many other new dynamics of coming out.

In decades past, people typically waited until they affirmed a concrete sexual identity before they considered disclosing their sexuality to others. Younger cohorts, particularly individuals under 22 years of age, are disclosing their sexualities prior to affirming a new sexual identity. That is, they are coming out with an *affinity* (i.e., "liking girls"), not a sexual identity (being gay, bisexual, etc.). Limited research has investigated these early roots of coming out. Another primary finding is that coming out is heavily influenced by an individual's gender presentation. Both gender conformity (e.g., a feminine female) and gender non-conformity (e.g., a masculine female) present unique challenges to coming out. Gender non-conformists are often "assumed gay," while gender conformists are assumed to be heterosexual. As a result, gender presentation can make coming out either more or less difficult—and the outcome has a great deal to do with what coming out means to each individual. These and other themes culminate in the summative finding that coming out remains a relevant, and highly influential, concept related to the formation and maintenance of sexual identities.

Coming out is a social construct that today garners a fair amount of empirical inquiry, yet rarely do researchers stop to question the usage and subsequent meanings of the concept itself. If you ask someone who is part of the sexual majority (i.e., heterosexual), "so, what is coming out all about?," they would likely tell you that it is the process by which people with "other" sexualities disclose their sexual identities to various people—parents, friends, coworkers, etc. If you were to query someone who has engaged in coming out, you would likely receive a response that includes the outward disclosure of a sexual identity, but you would just as likely hear stories of self-exploration, learning about one's own sexuality, and the development of acceptance or self-affirmation. The disconnect between popular, mainstream views of coming out and people's actual lived experiences with coming out can be attributed to a variety of factors including the proliferation of common storylines and media sensationalism which characterizes coming out as being an awkward, outward sharing of one's sexuality.

In order to understand the continued relevance of coming out and its role in contemporary society, we must consider the following fact: *coming out is a function of oppression.* Those groups which enjoy positions of privilege in society rarely, if ever, have to analyze, question, disclose, or justify the characteristics of their dominant traits. In the U.S., privilege is held by those who are white, male, cisgender[1] and—of import to this study—heterosexual (Kimmel and Ferber 2009). In the minds of the majority, to be heterosexual is to be *normal*. Conversely, to be gay, lesbian, bisexual, queer, fluid, pansexual, or polysexual is to be framed as the *other*. Heterosexuals often do not even consider their sexuality as a defining element in their self-identity (Herek 1990; Diamond 2008). It is simply not thought about. When a characteristic is normative it is rarely called into question. Heterosexuals do not feel the need to ask themselves "Why am I only interested in members of the other sex?" Quite simply, heterosexuality is everywhere. When something is normative it does not encourage introspection or explanation. It just *is*. But the maintenance of an LGBQ identity stands in juxtaposition to nearly everything we hear and see in society. Thus, the smallest inkling that one may be interested in members of the same sex lends itself to extensive self-exploration, and, if affirmed and desired by the individual, the outward disclosure of one's sexuality.

As a result of our heteronormative social arrangements, the common expectation is that everyone is "straight until proven gay." Even when someone does not provide proof of their sexuality via outward disclosure, many Americans believe they can detect sexual minorities by identifying those who violate traditional gender norms. It is no coincidence then that my choice of wording in the phrase above is eerily similarity to the legal phrase "innocent until proven guilty." After all, fear of judgment is one of the strongest barriers to coming out. This fear is derived from the constant barrage of heteronormative expectations that people receive from their family, their friends, their teachers, and various authority figures (Sears and Williams 1997). These expectations are in addition to the heteronormative wording and imagery seen across society from schools and churches to legal guidelines to the mass media.

Heteronormativity, in its most basic sense, is the presumption of heterosexuality as a universal fact among social arrangements. Heteronormativity frames "normal" romantic intimacy as shared only between people of different sexes (i.e., one male and one female). From an early age, people are bombarded by a multitude of messages concerning the heteronormative expectations of our society (Yep 2002). Martin and Kazyak (2009) noted the frequency with which children's G-rated films contain hetero-romantic love. Heteronormativity in children's media is not even reliant upon the presence of human characters. The animals in DreamWorks' *Madagascar* animated movies have hetero-romantic relationships, as do the cars in Disney Pixar's popular *Cars* franchise. Multiple participants in the current study noted the influence of children's media in forming negative self-images—in terms of both gender and sexuality. For example, Ari, an 18 year-old participant who identifies as a lesbian, spoke at length on the pervasive impact of Disney films. As she emphatically stated, "the things I internalized from watching Beauty and the Beast are what fucked me over the most in my life." Heteronormativity and traditional gender norms are conveyed through countless other media-based sources as well—books, magazines, advertisements, even nursery rhymes. Not surprisingly, the most frequently cited source of heteronormativity among most people is our central primary socialization unit: the family.

Family is often cited as one of the first—and consequently most influential—sources of heteronormative expectations (Savin-Williams 1998; Jenkins 2008). Most people who are born into two-parent households are brought up by a woman and a man, a mother and a father. Even those who are not raised in two-parent homes are typically raised in heterosexual households. To be fair, heterosexual households do not necessarily foster heteronormativity or homophobia—at least not intentionally. In fact, some family homes foster supportive environments that challenge the heterosexist underpinnings of social institutions and the broader society (Gorman-Murray 2008). Still, exposure to purely heterosexual social arrangements—among parents, extended family, neighbors—communicates a powerful message to a young, moldable mind—that one man plus one woman equals "normal."

Of the 30 participants in this study, 73 percent (22 out of 30) grew up in two-parent heterosexual households. Of those 22 people, 18 reported having intact families consisting of a biological mother and father who are still together, and another four grew up with mom and dad who are now separated (one of which is remarried). The percentage of people who grew up with intact families is higher than the U.S. average, and that is likely a result of the heavily middle-class sample in this study. Still the expectations of man and woman, husband and wife, mom and dad, boyfriend and girlfriend, were a daily reminder of what was expected of these individuals in their future relationships. And when social expectations fail to match up with personal lived experiences, an inner dialog begins—a dialog that oftentimes develops into various manifestations of coming out.

In her study of sexual fluidity among lesbians, Lisa Diamond (2008:58) aptly suggests, "the presumption of universal heterosexuality is so strong that [many women] never have to question it." The presumption of what Adrienne Rich (1980) calls "compulsory heterosexuality" is what makes coming out such an arduous journey for many LGBQ persons. To affirm an LGBQ identity is to go against everything an individual may have been socialized to believe or see as "normal"—that is, acceptable. It is essential, then, to recognize coming out as a social phenomenon rooted in the process of *doing difference* via sexuality.

Sexual identity formation and maintenance is a process of "describing one's social location within a changing social context" (Rust 1993:50). Scholars such as Paula Rust have therefore begun to recognize sexuality as something that is accomplished rather than purely innate.

Just as West and Zimmerman (1987) introduced the notion that gender is a routine accomplishment, so too is sexuality. Despite the revelation that gender and sexuality are quite social, the nature versus nurture argument continues to this day. Scholars such as Michael Kimmel (2008) have thwarted the "either/or" argument over the origins of gender and sexuality and replaced it with an "and/also" alternative. It's not a matter of nature versus nurture; it's how your nature is nurtured. As a result, literature on sexuality now emphasizes how sexual identities emerge from social interaction rather than focusing purely on innate personal characteristics. What we are left with is a new understanding of sexuality as a routine accomplishment embedded in everyday interaction. Sexual identities are less about expressing an essential truth and more about mapping out difference and diversity (Weeks 2003). West and Fenstermaker's (1995) concept of *doing difference* allows sexuality scholars to better investigate LGBQ interactions in everyday situations. It has contributed to our understanding of how LGBQ persons who wish to keep their sexual identities private must *do heteronormativity* in the workplace, in social situations, around family, or perhaps even as a part of one's own inner dialog. Although scholars such as Schilt and Westbrook (2009) challenge the necessity of doing heteronormativity, many LGBQ persons simply opt for the path of least resistance (Lucal 1999) which may consist of remaining closeted or perhaps passing as heterosexual in routine interaction.

In cases where LGBQ persons decide to forego sexual conformity, they may opt to engage in the self-affirmation of an LGBQ identity or the public expression of their sexuality—both of which constitute coming out. Like gender, sexuality emerges from social situations and serves as a means of legitimating the division of society on the basis of this characteristic. It is through social situations that we rationalize and duplicate our understanding of sexuality as a divisive characteristic. Power typically lies in the hands of the privileged, which in this case is the heterosexual majority. Stemming from the pre-1973 status of LGBQ persons as disordered, much about doing difference via sexuality (that is, *doing LGBQ*) is about shedding the past and working toward liberation. For some people this means inclusion, others separatism, and still others transcendence. Since heteronormativity purports that sexuality is synonymous with heterosexuality, for LGBQ persons there is no singular way to do sexuality except to do difference or undo heteronormativity. Indeed, many LGBQ persons are growing up without the use of a "closet" and are rather choosing to *do difference* from the very beginning (Seidman et al. 1999).

The idea of doing difference from the beginning (perhaps since adolescence), although progressive in its approach to sexuality, still involves the affirmation of a sexual identity that falls somewhere outside of heterosexuality. In this respect, even the most comfortable LGBQ person in the most affirming environment will engage in coming out—either inwardly or outwardly. As McCormack and Anderson (2010) emphasize, the influences of heteronormativity exist even in the most inclusive and affirming settings. As introduced in Chapter 2, coming out means different things to different people—but it has some sort of relevance to everyone. Despite the fact that "the closet" may no longer exist for some LGBQ persons, coming out (albeit in varying degrees) is still central to identity formation and maintenance. But coming out is different now than it was in decades past. Sexuality, like gender and race, is a social construct. Therefore, any concept related to sexuality is socially constructed as well. Coming out is a living social entity that morphs based on historical, political, and cultural change. Prior to delving further into exploration of the contemporary relevance of coming out, it is helpful to consider the origins of this relatively fluid concept.

A Brief History of Coming Out

During the Victorian era "coming out" referred to the ritual moment during which young affluent women were formally introduced to high society. The broad concept of "coming out" may have these Victorian roots, but its purpose and significance is far removed from these early origins. Fast forward to the 1920s and coming out began to refer to a less formal initiation of self-affirmed gay men into gay social life. As historian George Chauncey (1994) details, the early decades of the 20th century saw a definition of coming out that was rooted primarily in *entering the gay world*. It was during the early 20th century that we first saw the proliferation of sexual identities, including that of "heterosexual"—thus, sexuality became an increasingly divisive social trait. Between the 1920s and 1950s, most gay men and women in the U.S. lived a sexually bifurcated existence—split between work and leisure (among other boundaries). Coming out, then, was not about announcing one's sexuality to the heterosexual majority as much as it was becoming a part of "the club" among gay circles. "What was criminal was . . . denying [your sexual identity] to your sisters. Nobody cared about coming out to straights" (quoted in Chauncey 1994:276). This definition stands in stark contrast to modern-day conceptions of coming out which are framed just as much (if not more so) as *stepping away from the straight world.* That is, confirming to family and friends (and even oneself) that you are, in fact, "different."

Following commencement of the gay liberation movement—preceded by Stonewall—coming out increasingly encompassed the disclosure of one's sexuality to populations outside of the gay community (D'Emilio and Freedman 2012). Coming out became more of a public avowal—an act of resistance against oppression on the basis of sexuality. Thus, the goal of coming out shifted from that of a person's introduction to gay life into a political and social interaction aimed at challenging negative social meanings of homosexuality. The disclosure of one's sexual identity gained footing as young LGBQ men and women affirmed more publicly gay identities. Many men and women, previously engaged in "conventional" social arrangements (i.e., heterosexual relationships), were choosing to no longer deny their same-sex interests and thereby affirm LGBQ identities and subsequently come out to family and close friends as such. Coming out to family, friends, and even coworkers served the purpose of diffusing broad public fear associated with popular views of homosexuality.

As society progressed on into the 1990s and 2000s issues of sexuality entered the minds of the public more readily as relationship recognition debates sprang up around the country. During this climate of increased dialog, the public expression of one's sexuality grew from the occasional coming out story to a 1997 fever pitch centered on a two-part segment of the popular sitcom *Ellen.* The title character, played by Ellen DeGeneres, came out to family and friends as gay, thus affirming the popular notion that coming out is a matter of explaining sexual difference to other people. Fast forward to 2010, the year in which data for the current study was collected, and we saw a major public outpour of support for LGBQ youth with Dan Savage's "The It Gets Better Project." Primarily carried out via YouTube, It Gets Better provides an avenue to communicate broad public support and affirmation to even those LGBQ persons living in the least affirming environments. Indeed, the goal of coming out had broadened once again, to emphasize personal freedom, a general concern for the well-being of the individual, and the hope that bullying and intolerance would not relegate LGBQ youth to negative life outcomes.

When speaking of the history of coming out it is necessary to also discuss the metaphorical use of "the closet." Even among the participants in my research, "coming out" and "the closet" were often lumped together. Participants frequently touted how and when they "came out of the closet." In this sense, it is clear that these two terms can be mutually contributory. The closet presumably refers to the circumstance in which an individual is forced to hide his sexuality under a heterosexual visage. But as Seidman et al. (1999) pointedly confirms, many youth are growing up without ever feeling "closeted." The closet, in this sense, is a metaphor which explains the interaction of purposively hiding any element of one's sexual identity with the intention of preventing or subverting the negative reactions of other people. Despite asserting that we are moving beyond the closet, Seidman (2002) recognizes that, although the closet may be waning, it is nowhere near extinct. For this and other reasons (namely the continued pervasiveness of heteronormativity) coming out remains a significant element in the lives of most LGBQ persons. Although many participants in the current study did not speak specifically of being closeted (some did), they still regarded the realization that they are LGBQ and any subsequent sharing of their sexuality as coming out. So coming out is not contingent upon the existence or usage of a closet metaphor. Coming out has an impetus of its own, and it remains central to sexual identity formation and maintenance in contemporary society.

Purpose & Significance of the Study

Of all the literature concerning lesbian, gay, bisexual, and queer (LGBQ)[2] persons, coming out and the development of an LGBQ identity are probably the two best developed concepts (Shallenberger 1996). However, most studies on coming out are based on the assumption that "coming out" means the same thing to everyone, and that the entire experience is likely to fit a series of formulaic stages. The assumption of a shared, singular meaning for coming out is challenged in the present study. Is there a predictable and common "coming out" experience or does the meaning of, and experience associated with, coming out vary substantially from person to person?

A realistic construction of the meanings and experiences associated with coming out relies on a heavily inductive research methodology. In order to gain a fuller understanding of the experiences of LGBQ individuals, I worked diligently to abandon all assumptions and allow the unique narrative of each interviewee to emerge. Coming out is sociologically important. An improved understanding of coming out contributes to research on gender and sexuality. It also has the potential to improve the awareness and empathy of the general public on matters related to sexual orientation—a topic that is becoming increasingly salient in contemporary society. This project, then, is driven by what Denzin (1992) calls a critical pedagogy. The undercurrent of the research places emphasis on progressive politics and social justice, so it relies on an insistence that constructionism and postmodernism are mutually contributory.

Historically, much of the research on coming out has been directed at labeling stages in a "coming out process" (Cass 1979; Coleman 1982; Carrion and Lock 1997). The Cass model of coming out has served as the psychological foundation for understanding coming out for more than three decades. Even today Cass serves as the bedrock for myriad ally training programs around the country—aimed at helping straight allies understand what LGBQ persons experience when coming out. Thus, coming out is often positioned as a structured, formulaic process through which gay and lesbian persons will experience all or most of a series of stages, until the process is completed. Qualitative researchers have begun to move beyond such rigid structures by collecting and analyzing narratives of individuals' coming out in order to explore the uniqueness of people's experiences with coming out (Waldner and Magruder 1999; Merighi and Grimes 2000; Grierson and Smith 2005; Gorman-Murray 2008). Along with the increased openness with which researchers are approaching the topic, studies are also increasingly broadening the scope of sexuality beyond the typical gay/straight binary.

Research on coming out has made strides, but few studies emphasize learning about how coming out may be unique to each individual. By focusing only on general trends, social researchers inadvertently contribute to the trivialization of variations in the coming out experience. Layers of complexity and individuality get stripped down only to uncover the generic broad strokes that characterize a seemingly unified, monolithic experience of doing difference in a heteronormative society. Granted, overemphasizing the uniqueness of each individual's experiences would be just as detrimental as looking only for commonalities. My goal then is to locate the general in the particular while maintaining a watchful eye on the idiosyncratic variations that make coming out a highly individualized experience for each participant. The overall objective of this study is to provide a more nuanced, organic understanding of coming out as a general social phenomenon entered into and experienced by a wide array of people. It is a social phenomenon that, despite changing drastically over the past few decades, remains central to the lives of most LGBQ persons.

A few things should be said about the use of blanket terms such as "coming out." Seidman et al. (1999) asserts that the use of blanket concepts like "coming out" or "the closet" itself constructs LGBQ persons as suffering a common fate or similar circumstance. A postmodern take on the use of such categories or labels is that they are unfit to describe the varied life experiences of different people. An example of this shortcoming was encountered by Crawley and Broad (2004) in their study of lesbian, gay, bisexual and transgender (LGBT) community panels. Although community panels are intended to showcase the unique experiences of LGBT people, "the auspices of the setting and the coming-out formula story call on panelists to typify what it means to be LGBT, albeit in ways that contradict popular stereotypes" (Crawley and Broad 2004:39). So, although contemporary sexual identity categorization and storylines associated with coming out are intended to bring attention to individual variation, they still serve to undermine these very differences.

The study of coming out has implications that are much more far-reaching than simply advancing research agendas. The questions investigated by this study have the ability to promote a greater public understanding of the lives of LGBQ individuals in a time of heightened moral panic over matters of sexuality (Goode and Ben-Yehuda 2009). Numerous studies have hinted that much of the intolerance expressed toward sexual minorities comes from a simple lack of understanding and empathy. It is my hope that this research provides valuable insight into the meanings associated with coming out, what contemporary incarnations of coming out look like, and how the lives of everyday people are contorted by the social expectations tied to appeasing the sexual majority. Although this study is sociological in design and execution, the implications are relevant to all social sciences as well as individuals, groups and institutions in the public sphere.

Study Design

The current study takes a constructivist grounded theory approach to exploring coming out among lesbian, gay, bisexual, and queer individuals. Open-ended interviews were conducted in order to explore the meaning of coming out, and discern the ways in which coming out influences people's lives. All interviews were conducted face-to-face between August and December of 2010, and the duration of each interview ranged from 60 to 120 minutes. The entire research process (sampling, data collection, transcription, coding, analyses, and write-ups) was completed by me.

Most research maintains a decidedly narrow focus on coming out, scrutinizing a single, predetermined element of coming out (e.g., the influence of family formation or one's own religiosity on coming out). Beyond exploring the meanings of coming out, the major themes included in this volume were all extracted theoretically from the participants' narratives. I did not set out to "unearth" these particular themes via specific questions or any a priori theory. Rather than self-imposing a series of finite research questions or hypotheses, I employed a very open set of interview questions and relied upon the interview data to dictate the results of the study. My analysis is informed by symbolic interactionism, and guided by constructivist grounded theory—which was employed for my organization, coding, and analysis (Charmaz 2006). Symbolic interactionism and constructivist grounded theory both maintain a focus on the creation and evolution of meaning. The goal then, in terms of employing an interactionist perspective on coming out, is to understand the socially situated meaning of the concept (i.e., coming out) at a given moment in order to investigate how it shapes individuals' lived experiences.

A total of 30 participants were included in this study. This sample size was instrumental in allowing me to gather rich data on the meaning of coming out as well as other themes that arose during my grounded analyses. Participants for this study were recruited by employing both snowball and purposive sampling techniques. Considering the methodological challenges of obtaining a diverse sample of LGBQ individuals, most of which have taken their sexual identities public to some extent, snowball sampling is the most viable sampling choice. Snowball samples, although ideal for recruiting highly "invisible" populations, are associated with a variety of methodological concerns, not the least of which is potential homogeneity (Groves 2009). For example, referrals from a single LGBQ organization would be likely to share many traits with one another. But, by initiating 4-5 different trails of snowballing, I worked to minimize this effect and reach populations who may not be accessible through any other means. It is standard research practice to use pseudonyms to protect the participants, a fact that I explained at the beginning of each interview. To my surprise, many of my participants insisted that I use their actual names as opposed to pseudonyms. For those who chose to utilize pseudonyms, all notations made during these interviews included no mention of their actual names.

Most studies on coming out emphasize a specific segment of the population such as adolescents, college students, young professionals, or people in mid-adulthood. These sorts of samples allow researchers to make more direct within-group comparisons; however, they limit the investigation of coming out as a general social phenomenon entered into and experienced by people from all walks of life. Collecting data across multiple dimensions allows for greater representativeness and it helps capture the overall texture of the topic (Corsaro 1985). Historically, participants in studies on coming out tended to be white, highly educated, and of a high socioeconomic status (Griffith and Hebl 2002). In an effort to minimize the homogeneity of the sample I employed some purposive sampling techniques which were directed at gaining diversity on the basis of gender, race, education, sexual orientation, age, and "degree of outness."

Early on in the process of collecting data a sharp distinction emerged between two groups of participants and their modes of coming out—those born prior to 1988 (over 22 at the time of interview), and those born after 1988 (22 and under at the time of interview). Since marked differences appeared during the course of my data collection that really begged further exploration, I chose to engage in some theoretical sampling in terms of participants' age and another characteristic ("degree of outness"). Considering the small sample size in this study, the birth year of 1988 is not a precise cut point. Nonetheless, recognition of cohort-based trends led to some theoretical sampling in order to obtain a large segment of the sample on each side of this artificial divide. Other than providing a basis of comparison, participants born prior to 1988 are not frequently discussed in the current study. Most themes included in this volume (i.e., the new dynamics of coming out) relate specifically to the participants under 22 years of age at the time of interview (2010).

Simply put, younger populations are growing up in an environment of increasingly open dialog concerning sexuality (especially since 1993, when the Hawai'i marriage case of Baehr v. Lewin launched relationship recognition into the social spotlight) and this came through in the data. I completed my data collection with 10 participants over the age of 25, and 20 participants under 25 enabled—thus enabling me to further explore the contemporary meanings of coming out, and gain more insight on recent developments in identity formation and maintenance. Although many of the themes included in this volume rely heavily on the experiences of these younger participants, the data provided by older cohorts provided important information on the broader context of coming out—thus allowing me to better engage in understanding how coming out is changing.

A well-rounded depiction of coming out required that I obtain a sample that includes individuals who have only come out to one or two people, as well as individuals who have come out to a greater degree. Research is lacking on those who have just begun to come out, so these individuals offer the unique opportunity to learn about coming out as a fresh and emergent theme in their lives. So in addition to sampling individuals who were quite young, I also sought participants who were early in their coming out—regardless of age (snowball sampling does not afford me the luxury of reaching individuals who were out to nobody but themselves).

Although I engaged in this study with the intention of exploring coming out as a general social endeavor, due to my limited sample size, and my decision to utilize snowball sampling, my findings cannot be generalized to all persons who engage in coming out. Also, despite my best efforts, the sample lacks any participants who identify as black and/or presently identifies as bisexual (for a discussion of sampling challenges, please reference the Appendix). Still, considering the breadth of participants in my sample, I am confident that my data accounts for a great many of the types of experiences that LGBQ persons may encounter while coming out.

Participant Characteristics

There is a fair amount of diversity among the 30 participants in this study. The sample is diverse in terms of age, gender, race, sexual orientation, education, and social class (see Table 1.1). The mean age of participants is 26 years of age, while the median age is closer to 24. Although more diverse than most studies on coming out, the racial/ethnic composition of my sample still lacks the degree of diversity sought. Important to note is that I did not impose a specified list of racial/ethnic identities from which participants had to choose. I opted instead to allow participants to define their race and ethnicity in their own verbiage and on their own terms. This same logic was followed for sexual orientation, social class, and religion. Considering how most studies on coming out are about 90 percent white, the participants in this sample are relatively racially and ethnically diverse. Of the 30 participants, 18 are White, 4 Latino, 2 Bi-racial, 2 Jewish, 1 Indian, 1 Muslim Arab, 1 Mediterranean, and 1 Viking. Markedly absent are any participants who identified as African American or Caribbean American—both populations which are underserved in research on sexual identities. Throughout data collection I made a concerted effort to locate and interview black participants, but these potential interviewees ultimately chose not to participate. This unfortunate outcome encouraged me to focus my next major research project exclusively on African American and Caribbean American participants (a project which is currently underway).

Table 1.1 - Participant Characteristics

NAME	AGE	GENDER	RACE	SEXUAL IDENTITY	EDUC.	CLASS	RELIGION
Cindy	27	Woman	White/ Italian	Lesbian	B.A.	Middle	None
Athena	54	Woman	White/ Irish	Lesbian	Ph.D.	Middle	Christian
Renee	29	Woman	White	Lesbian	M.A.	Middle	None
H.G.	52	Man	White	Queer	M.B.A.	Middle	Christian
Ram	21	Man	Indian	Gay	Some College	Lower-Middle	None
Ari	28	Woman	Latina/ Mestiza	Lesbian	B.A.	Middle	None
Janice	22	Woman	Peruvian	Lesbian	Some College	Middle	Agnostic
Jim	46	Man	Caucasian/ White	Gay	Ph.D.	Middle	Quaker
Ruby	24	Woman/ Fluid	Sicilian/ Mediteran.	Does Not Identify	B.A.	Middle	Zen Buddhist
Eden	22	Woman	White	Does Not Identify	Some College	Lower-Middle	Spiritual
Kelly	22	Woman	Caucasian	Pansexual	B.S.	Middle	None
Kyle	21	Woman	Viking	Lesbian	Some College	Middle	None
Richard	24	Man	Caucasian	Gay	B.A.	Upper Middle	Atheist
Brian	20	Man	White	Queer	Some College	Middle	None
Carly	22	Woman	White	Queer	Some College	Middle	None
Rachel	20	Woman	Jewish/ Caucasian	Gay	Some College	Middle-Upper	Agnostic
Arielle	24	Woman	Israeli	Lesbian	B.A.	Middle	Jewish (culturally)
Michelle	25	Woman	Irish/ Mexican	Gay	B.A.	Middle	None

Gabrielle	22	Woman	Latino	Lesbian	Some College	Wealthy	Agnostic (culturally Jewish)
Alex	24	Woman	White	Gay	B.A.	Middle	None
Nathan	21	Man	Bi-racial	Gay	Some College	Upper Middle	Christian: non-denom.
Veronica	20	Woman/ Fluid	Caucasian	Lesbian	Some College	Middle	Jewish
Brandon	19	Man	White	Gay	Some College	Lower- Middle	Agnostic (Humanist)
Adam	20	Man	White	Gay	Some College	Lower Class	Roman Catholic
Hannah	18	Woman	White	Gay	High School	Middle	Jewish
Lee	20	Man	White	Gay	Some College	Middle	Agnostic
Pao	24	Woman	Latino	Gay	B.A.	Middle	Agnostic
Steve	32	Man	White	Gay	High School	Middle	Agnostic
Chris	26	Man	White	Gay	High School	Lower- Middle	None
Hamed	30	Man	Muslim Arab	Gay	Some College	Upper Middle	Muslim (non- prac)

The sample consists of 12 men and 18 women (two of which maintain a decidedly fluid gender identity). In terms of their present sexual orientation, 15 participants identify as gay, 9 as lesbians, 3 as queer, 1 as fluid, 1 as pansexual, and 2 prefer not to identify. As noted above, none of the participants identified as bisexual at the time of interview (although many had previously identified as such). Participants' "degree of outness," ranged from individuals who had shared their sexuality with only two or three people all the way up to those who considered themselves "completely out." As is the case with other studies on coming out, this sample is highly educated. I could suggest that highly educated people are more likely to be surrounded by an affirming environment or that highly educated people are simply more apt to speak of their experiences—but these assertions are both merely conjecture at this point. Rather than having an overabundance of people with high upper-class standing, the average participant in this study is decidedly middle class. Although the modal group (12 people) consisted of those who designated "no religion," this sample still yielded a fair amount of religious diversity—and some high levels of religiosity as well.

All participants lived within two hours of Orlando, Florida at the time of their interviews. As a region, Central Florida proved to be ideal for conducting this study. The region is home to two major Metropolitan Statistical Areas (MSAs) in Orlando and Tampa, as well as countless suburbs, small towns and unincorporated settlements. Generally speaking, the size of any particular Florida community has a lot to say about the quantity and types of LGBQ resources as well as gay spaces that are available. Tampa and Orlando have fairly well-established gay communities; while smaller towns like Winter Garden and St. Cloud have little to no LGBQ resources at all. The region is also home to two large research universities and a variety of highly-regarded liberal arts colleges—each of which contributes to a vibrant and growing LGBQ community. Collectively, the characteristics of Central Florida add up to an eclectic mix of social environments that were experienced and subsequently discussed by the 30 participants in this study.

The Plan of the Book

This opening chapter was centered on providing a framework for investigating the concept of coming out. The major takeaway is that, in order to understand coming out, you must first comprehend the concept of heteronormativity and highlight its influence on sexual identity formation and maintenance among sexual minorities. This seemingly simple social fact is central to the analyses found in the remaining chapters. The remainder of the book is structured around the major themes that emerged from my interview data on coming out.

People often discuss "coming out" as a concept which has a singular, shared meaning. Even social scientists typically equate its meaning to the public disclosure of one's sexual identity. In reality, the meaning of coming out varies substantially from person to person. Chapter 2 provides an organic look at the various meanings that participants in my research attribute to coming out. Meanings include coming out to oneself (self-affirmation), coming out to family/friends, and coming out as full disclosure (and oftentimes a combination of two or more of the above). The two most significant findings in this chapter are that 1) coming out is indeed still a relevant concept, and 2) coming out is not always an external endeavor. The realization that, for some people, coming out is entirely a matter of self-affirmation problematizes research which frames coming out as being entirely about outward disclosure.

An extensive body of literature exists with regard to why an individual may choose not to come out. Studies often cite the influence of family and friends, social norms, or even refusal on the part of the individual to affirm an LGBQ identity. However, rarely does research entertain how these same three social influences alter the way in which an individual *does* come out. Most people grow up under the impression that to be straight is to be "normal." Influences from outside (family, friends, media, etc.) as well as inside (oneself) encourage those who have same-sex attractions to feel that they must somehow hold on to heterosexuality—at least to a degree. Chapter 3 focuses on ten participants in this study, each of whom engaged in a queer apologetic— coming out as bisexual despite being interested only in members of the same sex. The queer apologetic is essentially a form of identity compromise whereby an individual discloses a bisexual identity that she feels will be palatable to her family, friends, or even herself. This compromise is based on the rationale that bisexuality simultaneously satisfies 1) her personal attractions to only members of the same sex, and 2) society's expectation that she be attracted to members of the other sex. The queer apologetic exemplifies the struggle to affirm an LGBQ identity in a heteronormative society. It also helps explain the difficulty in maintaining a bisexual identity (or any other "intermediate" identify, for that matter).

Building upon the foundation established in the first three chapters, Chapter 4 covers a series of interactions, each of which establishes coming out as a concept that is undergoing massive transformation. The most revolutionary facet of this chapter is a subsection on "coming out with affinity, not identity." Most sexuality research is restricted to people who have affirmed concrete sexual identities, but my data demonstrates that many people initiate coming out prior to affirming an LGBQ identity. They come out first as "liking boys/girls" (i.e., a sexual affinity), and little to no research has investigated these early roots of coming out. Other topics included in this chapter are the tendency of people to shift identities over time (which often prompts people to "reset" their coming out) and the proliferation of progressive identities such as pansexual, polysexual, fluid, and open. For the most part, research on coming out has been limited to lesbian, gay, and bisexual populations, so these newer identities are fertile ground for sociological inquiry.

Research at the intersection of gender and sexuality is underdeveloped on the influence of gender presentation on coming out. Chapter 5 begins with a thorough review of the relationship between sex, gender, and sexuality—a necessary for understanding how gender affects coming out. The chapter details how both gender conformity (e.g., a feminine female) and gender non-conformity (e.g., a masculine female) present unique challenges to coming out. For starters, the influence of gender presentation on coming out varies from person to person. For some, gender conformity lightens the load for coming out broadly because many acquaintances and peers assume that they are straight. For other people, gender conformity makes coming out more difficult because they have to make a more concerted effort to come out to others—again, because other people assume them to be straight based on their gender presentation. Conversely, gender non-conformists may experience greater ease coming out broadly because they are "assumed gay," but they also often experience greater opposition from family and friends who resist gender non-conformity. In many ways, family and friends are more willing to affirm a non-normative sexual identity than they are to accept what they perceive to be a violation of traditional gender norms. Individual variation in the perceived effects of gender presentation on coming out has a great deal to do with what coming out means to each individual, so this chapter does a nice job of tying the current topic back into material from previous chapters (particularly Chapter 2).

Coming out is frequently talked about as a point-in-time event as well as a gradual process. However, evidence provided in Chapter 6 suggests that coming out is not merely a process—rather, it is a career. This may seem like simple semantics, but it is so much more. The conceptions of coming out as a "gradual process" or as "a career" are similar in that they both recognize coming out as an ongoing progression. However, there is a sharp distinction between these two perspectives of coming out. A process is eventually completed. The uniqueness of the career perspective of coming out is the position that coming out is never entirely completed. It is a recognition that, as long as sexual minorities are "othered" in society, members of the LGBQ community will continuously have to engage in coming out. Even people who live in LGBQ affirming environments are faced with meeting new people and forming new relationships (personal, professional, etc.) which makes coming out a perpetually influential element in people's lives.

The final chapter (Chapter 7) begins with a brief synopsis of the findings discussed throughout the first six chapters. Much of this chapter is directed at reflecting on the results of the study and asking the questions: "What does this mean?" and "Where do we go from here?" This concluding chapter also provides some applied suggestions for researchers, service providers, and LGBQ groups, as well as individuals. Finally, I conclude by offering insight into some other trends that were indicated by the data, yet in need of further inquiry. Other avenues for future research will be discussed as well.

As I discussed briefly above, I utilized constructivist grounded theory as the bedrock of this study. The unique feature of constructivist grounded theory is that it recognizes how data is created through the mutual contributions of researcher and participant. Such a perspective has encouraged me to engage in reflection through constant note-taking and retrospective analysis of my research methods. A lot of energy was put into issues related to reactivity, bias, and the social/political environment during which my interviews took place. All of these elements of my research methodology led to the accumulation of insight that is valuable in its own right. This material is compiled into a relatively brief Appendix which further contextualizes the research project for interested readers. I find this sort of appendix extremely helpful in terms of getting inside the mind of the researcher and realizing the many idiosyncrasies that have an impact on the direction and findings of the study.

---

[1] "Cisgender" refers to individuals whose sex (female/male) matches the gender they were assigned at birth (girl/boy, woman/man) as well as their personal identity (Schilt and Westbrook 2009). Cisgender is commonly used as a compliment to transgender.

[2] Although this study is designed around the use of these labels, study participants may very well identify as lesbian, gay, bisexual, queer, questioning, pansexual, poly-sexual, fluid, or they may prefer to abstain from attaching any such label to their sexuality. Essentially, my sampling frame included anyone who engages in a process of coming out related to their sexual orientation, so the participants need not self-identify as LGBQ.

2

The Meaning(s) of Coming Out

For me, coming out is accepting *me*, accepting who I am—I'm gay, that's it. Telling myself—not really coming "out." I just find that so cliché that people think that coming out is just practically making a speech, like "hey everybody . . ." Not really. Coming out is me accepting me—nobody else, just me.

~ Pao

Based on the meaning that Pao attributes to her coming out in this opening quote, some readers might think to themselves "but that's not coming out." And they would not be alone in this declaration. The majority of social and behavioral research on coming out refers to it as a process rooted in the *disclosure* of one's sexuality—the outward disclosure, that is. In fact, studies on coming out are centered almost exclusively on people "telling," "sharing," or "disclosing" their sexual difference. Of all the literature concerning LGBQ persons, coming out is purported to be one of the best developed concepts (Shallenberger 1996). However, most studies on coming out are based on the assumption that "coming out" means the same thing across individuals. Further, it is assumed by much of the psychological community that the experiences associated with coming out are likely to fit a series of formulaic stages (Savin-Williams 2001). But coming out is not a simple linear, goal-oriented, developmental process (Rust 1993), and the experiences associated with coming out are as numerous as the LGBQ people who have engaged in coming out.[1]

Pao's explanation of coming out being an entirely internal endeavor represents a challenge to traditional models of coming out. Sociological research is still underdeveloped in terms of taking a more inductive approach to exploring the unique experiences of those with an LGBQ identity. Even qualitative studies that employ an objectivist take on grounded theory typically assume that respondents share their meanings (Charmaz 2000). As long as research relies on the assumption that coming out means the same thing to everyone, how can we really begin to explore individual variations in all things related to coming out?

The ambiguity of meanings related to matters of sexuality is not a new phenomenon. In her book *Virginity Lost*, sociologist Laura Carpenter (2005) set out to investigate virginity loss as a cultural phenomenon that is important to study in its own right. To her surprise, Carpenter quickly came to recognize that perhaps the most challenging element of her study was the dearth of research on the *meaning* of virginity loss:

> Once I began to research the topic, I found that the scholarship on early sexuality was largely silent on the meaning of virginity loss, and even more so about its definition. This silence surprised me, given how consistently American institutions—mass media, medical science, schools, religious institutions, public policy organizations, and the government—depicted virginity loss as one of, if not *the*, most meaningful events in an individual's sexual career (Carpenter 2005:5).

By simply rereading Carpenter's passage while replacing the term "virginity loss" with "coming out," we see that the rest of her statement seems to hold true. Coming out is often touted as central to identity formation, and its relevance is echoed throughout American institutions, yet we have exerted little effort on discerning the meaning of the concept. Most often coming out is framed heterocentrically as being entirely about disclosing difference.

Aside from a recent publication of my own (Guittar 2013a), I have yet to identify a single study where one of the primary research questions is focused on exploring the meaning of coming out. Fortunately, by scrutinizing the details of previous studies, it is possible to construct somewhat of a mosaic of meanings that have been attributed to coming out. Some of these meanings are extracted from the narratives of participants within the given studies, although most of them are definitions proffered by researchers at the onset of their manuscripts. For example, according to Waldner and Magruder (1999), coming out refers simply to the acknowledgement of a gay identity to others. A slightly more specific rendition of this was shared by Merighi and Grimes (2000) who summarized coming out as the disclosure of one's sexuality to family members. These studies, along with others (Griffith and Hebl 2002; Johnston and Jenkins 2003; McLean 2007), typically maintain that coming out includes 1) disclosure of a sexual identity, 2) the involvement of family, friends, or coworkers, and 3) a transformative nature to the exchange. However, overly simplistic definitions of coming out do not take into account that, among other things, coming out means sharing one's history and "working to avoid stereotypic clarity about the messier parts of [ones'] lives" (Crawley 2009:214).

Considering the variation in definitions, it is essential that we gain an understanding of how those individuals who are engaged in coming out define this concept. Appleby (2001) offers a unique approach to defining the concept. Rather than proposing an explanation for what coming out means, he refrains from disclosing a meaning aside from speaking about a theme extracted from his ethnographic interview data: that coming out is an ongoing process. Although a meaning of coming out is never explicitly stated, the author alludes to coming out only as the outward disclosure of one's sexual orientation. Still, he at least gives the participants leeway to define coming out as an ongoing process. Unfortunately, few studies have offered participants this opportunity to contribute their own input into the conceptualization of the term "coming out."

Some researchers altogether avoid defining the concept. For example, in his studies on coming out to parents, Savin-Williams (1989; 1998) discusses how the disclosure of one's sexuality to family members is a pivotal and often neglected part of the process, yet an explicit definition of coming out is not completely stated. In his work, there is occasional mention of how the psychological community relies on a rigid definition of coming out (Savin-Williams 2001). However, he rebukes such a practice citing how it does not adequately explain most individuals' lived experiences. Perhaps the lack of a definition in his writings is simply a reflection of how the author wishes to avoid placing a definitive label on people's rather unique experiences related to sexual orientation and identity.

Still, many researchers rely on their own definitions of coming out while interviewing LGBQ persons. In a study of young lesbian and bisexual women, Oswald (1999:66) states that "coming out is a process of significant change for women who accept and disclose bisexual or lesbian identities, and for those to whom they come out." Although Oswald's definition is an example of circumventing the question of what coming out means and defining it for oneself, her definition of coming out is unique in that it explains coming out as both self-acceptance and public disclosure. Oswald (1999:67) later states how each participant in her study "was interviewed about how she *came out to herself* and the most important people in her life" (emphasis added). Oswald's statement begs the question of whether self-acceptance alone might even constitute coming out. Or perhaps self-acceptance is simply a prerequisite to coming out as opposed to being part of the process.

At some juncture we need to stop and ask ourselves if the meaning we ascribe to a concept is similar to the meanings held by individuals outside of academia. In the case of coming out, this remains to be seen as very few studies have given participants the opportunity to weigh in on its meaning. Granted, some studies on coming out are written by scholars who themselves identify as having an LGBQ identity. In these cases, it is possible that the researchers simply use the definition that most aptly describes their own experiences. This is an approach most often used in autoethnographic works of coming out at work or school. Since the author is the central figure in these narratives, it makes sense to use one's own definition of coming out (see: Coming Out in the Higher Education Classroom, a special feature in *Feminism and Psychology* 2009).

As for studies where the researcher is interviewing or surveying a chosen population, the question remains: is the author's definition of coming out in congruence with that held by each of the participants? Scholarship in research methodology has devoted a great deal of time and effort to investigating how researchers and study participants construct different meanings of a concept or question (Groves et al. 2009). In many cases there remains an assumption of shared meaning between the researcher and the participants. This assumption of shared meaning even permeates many carefully constructed qualitative studies that use various incarnations of grounded theory in their coding and analysis (Charmaz 2000). This brings me back to the question at hand: What does coming out mean to different people? Does telling a close friend constitute coming out, or is it a matter of disclosing one's sexual orientation to a parent? Is it a matter of full disclosure to all family, friends, and acquaintances? Does self-acceptance constitute coming out? Does one ever truly come out?

Assumptions by researchers about the meaning of coming out may typify people's experiences in ways that are not true to individuals' lived experiences. Such assumptions and vagaries are problematic in terms of gaining a better understanding of what coming out really means to individuals. In reviewing the literature on coming out, the only conclusion I have come to is that perhaps there are so many definitions for coming out simply because "coming out" is not a concept with a singular, shared meaning. Through the use of constructivist grounded theory I dig below the surface of typical "storytold" meanings and work with participants to uncover meanings that are relevant to their social worlds.

The Meanings of Coming Out

> The way I define coming out is coming out to my parents because everyone I met and talked to, you know, my colleagues, my professors, my friends, they all knew I was queer. But, my parents never knew.

> ~ Ari

At the onset of this study, I set out to discover what "coming out" means to individuals in the LGBQ community. In the most general sense, coming out is often compared to *telling* or *storytelling*. For example, in the case of mental health patients, individuals often must often engage in the telling of their condition—such as in the workplace or around new friends (Goffman 1974). Some participants in the current study even used the word "telling" in discussing their coming out experiences. For example, Ram, a 21 year-old gay man, discussed how he became "addicted to telling." As he explained, "every little person I told I feel like a knot was undone." Or as stated by Gabrielle, a 22 year-old lesbian, "coming out is a way of telling others who you are." Coming out, or even telling, therefore assumes that there is something that needs disclosing, something that requires sharing. Taken one step further, it also implies that there currently exists a certain level of secrecy around a particular topic (hence the analogy of "the closet").

Scholars such as Seidman et al. (1999) emphasize that contemporary identity disclosure is less focused on legitimating sexualities via coming out since non-heterosexual identities are becoming increasingly normalized. That is, LGBQ persons are less likely to experience secrecy and social isolation, so "the closet" is not as repressive as it once was. The normalization of LGBQ identities casts doubt on the relevance of coming out as a necessary part of identity formation and maintenance. However, every single participant in this study acknowledged engaging in coming out. Evidence from my interviews challenges the notion that coming out is no longer a relevant concept. Coming out is a personal and social process that appears to be omnipresent so long as we operate within a heteronormative society. As seen in the opening quote, the face of coming out may be changing. Many teens and young adults are assumed gay in certain contexts. The *assumption* that someone is gay is oftentimes based on physical identifiers that are stereotypically associated with gay culture or a gender presentation based in gender non-conformity (e.g., a masculine female). But, even those who are assumed to be gay still engage in some form of coming out.

What is Coming Out?

Across the body of research on coming out we have already seen that substantial variability exists in the *meaning* of coming out. If there is variability in the meaning attached to coming out within academia, then it is likely that there is variability among its use within the LGBQ community too—and this study serves as evidence of such. It should come as no surprise then that even the word "meaning" has multiple interpretations. For example, when asked: "What does coming out *mean* to you?" my respondents interpreted the word "meaning" differently, yielding a variety of responses. I set out to learn more about what coming out means to each individual (i.e., what coming out entails). One participant, Eden, proceeded to tell me somewhat philosophically how coming out means "to live life openly and honestly." Many other individuals started by defining the term broadly (as in a definition) and then explaining how it relates to their lives. Throughout the interviews some resounding themes emerged such as coming out to oneself, coming out to family/friends, and coming out as full disclosure, among others.

Coming Out to Oneself

One of the most ignored elements of coming out is whether or not "coming out to oneself" is part of the equation. Some scholars maintain that self-acceptance or self-affirmation is part of coming out—the popular Cass (1979) model of coming out explains it as such. But, if coming out is the *public* disclosure of one's sexual identity (as many scholars posit), then logic would dictate that self-acceptance—an internal process—must be a prerequisite for coming out rather than a part of coming out. As one participant, Athena, put it, "you have to come in to yourself before you come out to others." Athena seems to be indicating self-acceptance as a prerequisite to coming out. However, she later recognized that although her vision of coming out does include the public disclosure of her identity to others, coming out "has more to do with accepting yourself than other people accepting you." Based much of the data in this study, self-acceptance is quite central to coming out and not merely a prerequisite.

Across many interviews, the discussion of coming out to oneself was an emergent trend. Not only were participants discussing the importance of self-acceptance, but in some cases they were referring to self-acceptance as being synonymous with coming out. Pao, a 24 year-old woman who identifies as gay, mirrors this sentiment that self-affirmation *is* coming out.

> For me, coming out is accepting *me*, accepting who I am—I'm gay, that's it. Telling myself - not really coming out. I just find that so cliché that people think that coming out is just practically making a speech, like "hey everybody . . ." Not really. Coming out is me accepting me—nobody else, just me.

Incidentally, with the exception of her sister, Pao has not come out to any of her family. But, she does intend to. It is just that the disclosure of her sexuality to her family is not a defining element of her coming out story, nor is it a part of what coming out means to her.

Another participant, Kelly, agreed that, at least for her, coming out means purely coming out to oneself.

> Coming out, in terms of myself, would probably be me accepting myself for loving who I want to love and not doing what society tells me—you know, like, loving who I *should* love. That, to me, is coming out. There are other definitions, you know, like telling people about it, but that's never been something I've felt like I've had to do only because I was lucky and I knew I would have support no matter what.

Kelly was very careful in qualifying why self-acceptance was synonymous with coming out for her, but why coming out likely has a broader meaning for other people. In her evaluation, self-acceptance is more central to her coming out since she has such strong external support from others. Kelly's family had been proactive in letting her know that she would be loved regardless of her sexual orientation, and they conveyed this through concrete action. Kelly describes a phone call she received from her mother during her first year of college—while Kelly was still unsure about her sexuality. "She's like 'Kelly, are you a lesbian or what? Do I need to, like, buy you a coming out cake or something?' It really was awesome. I knew that if I ever . . ." Kelly conveyed that, from that point forward, she took solace in her family's support and looked at her coming out as purely a personal journey of self-acceptance.

More common in the current study was the inclusion of "coming out to oneself" as one element in a broader meaning that individuals ascribed to coming out. Self-acceptance was frequently depicted as an initial step in coming out. In fact, of the 30 participants in the sample, exactly half of them (15) indicated coming out to oneself as being a central element in their meanings of coming out. Most participants were very clear that coming out to oneself was not a prerequisite to coming out; rather, it was a major part of coming out—of the process itself. Even though most agreed that coming out to oneself was part of the process, there was some disagreement. For example, Carly, a 22 year-old female who identifies as queer, spoke of coming out to oneself as both a part of the process and a prerequisite:

> Coming out to yourself is part of the process. I know people who, on a regular basis, sleep with people of the same gender, yet do not even think to themselves that they can be anything other than straight. I don't get that at all, but I feel like that's an important part of, yeah, coming out to yourself. I think of it as a prerequisite.

Veronica, a 20 year-old who identifies as a lesbian, embodied the notion that coming out means both 1) coming out to oneself, and 2) coming out to others. As Veronica put it, "coming out, I think, for me . . . it's two steps—coming out to yourself, which was the hardest step, for me—and coming out to the people in your life . . . letting them know who you are." Veronica's discussion of these two elements to coming out went well beyond this single statement. As was the case with other participants who saw coming out to oneself as one part of a broader meaning to coming out, she discussed it often. In fact, her reference to a two-prong meaning came up organically earlier in our interview before I delved into any questions on the meaning of coming out.

> I just came out with it to Matty [one of her close guy friends]. I had come out to myself probably the—well, kind of—like, I didn't let it process all the way. I had kind of come out to myself probably the same week because I was trying to be, like, the aspiring psychology major in high school and I sat myself down in front of a mirror and I, whenever I had a breakdown—sometimes I do that—I'll just vent almost to myself and go on an uncensored rant, and it slipped out of my mouth that I'd fallen in love with all of these people, these girls, in my past, and I mean it was out there but it was like my brain was still fighting it a little bit until I hung out with Matty and I just said it, and once it was out there it was just like {whistling sound} free. And, then from that point I told a couple of other people.

Here Veronica conveys not only that the meaning of coming out has two elements, but that they combine to create a sense of having truly come out. Coming out to herself gave her the confidence to come out to Matty, but self-acceptance alone was not enough to constitute the meaning she ascribes to coming out. Veronica did not feel as if coming out was a completed process at that point. Still, from that moment forward she had a sense that her coming out was becoming familiar, comfortable, and progressive. Coming out to herself verbally in the mirror made it real, and telling Matty made coming out a symbol of liberation.

Another clear example of coming out to oneself as part of the larger meaning attributed to coming out came from Brandon, a 19 year-old gay male. As Brandon saw it, coming out is "a three-step process." He spoke first about how coming out means "coming out within and having that self-realization of your sexuality." Following this realization, there is "an initial disclosing of your sexual identity to those around you—your peers, people you go to school with." Then, he lastly spoke about "the disclosing of your identity where the topic just happens to specifically come up." So, the meaning Brandon attributes to coming out goes one step further than Veronica in that he alludes to coming out as an ongoing, unending process driven by new circumstances and new situations. But both Veronica and Brandon shared the sentiment held by many participants in this study: coming out to oneself is part of the meaning of coming out, but self-acceptance alone does not account for the entire meaning of coming out.

Coming out to oneself was central to the meaning of coming out more often for individuals who identified their sexual orientation as queer, fluid, pansexual, or open. Research suggests that coming out is more of a necessity for people who are interested only in members of the same sex (i.e., gay or lesbian) than for bisexuals (McLean 2007). In the case of bisexuality or various progressive identities (e.g., pansexual, fluid), individuals are not as easily identifiable on the basis of with whom they engage in relationships. Considering our society's insistence on binary logic (gay/straight, male/female) those who have attractions for both men and women, multiple genders, or those who do not use gender as a determinate for choosing a mate are often misunderstood (Lucal 2008). Western societies' socially constructed, dualistic framework makes coming out more problematic for individuals who are bisexual, queer, fluid or pansexual. For example, a bisexual woman who is currently engaged in a relationship with another woman will be perceived as gay—that is, bisexuality cannot be understood by a single situational observation. Such realities make the public disclosure of one's sexuality less central to the meaning of coming out.

Coming Out to Others

Aside from the two participants whose meanings of coming out were rooted only in coming out to oneself, every other participant shared a meaning for coming out that included some form of coming out to others. I should qualify this statement by mentioning that the term "coming out to others" was not found in any of my interviews. Rather, it is a useful way for me to encompass the two most common themes outside of coming out to oneself: 1) coming out to family/friends, and 2) coming out as "full disclosure." These two elements of coming out both include the disclosure of one's sexuality to another person (i.e., coming out to others). The interviews of a select few participants included mention of both coming out to family/friends and coming out as full disclosure. But, for the most part, participants mentioned only one or the other. Those participants who cited coming out as full disclosure mentioned very little about coming out to family/friends in discussing the meaning of coming out. This finding likely has to do with the methodological differentiation between a necessary cause and a sufficient cause. Coming out to family/friends is a necessary cause for full disclosure, while full disclosure is a sufficient cause for coming out to family and friends. So, those who talked about coming out as meaning full disclosure inferentially provided sufficient cause for coming out to family/friends.

One important item to remember here is that I am not concerned so much with to whom individuals do or do not disclose their sexuality or in which social arena. I am concerned with *what coming out means to each individual*. Although the discussion of meaning often includes details related to whom they chose to disclose their sexuality and in what setting, individuals having disclosed their sexuality to family/friends does not automatically imply that their meaning of coming out includes coming out to family/friends. Such was demonstrated by Kelly above in the section on coming out to oneself. Kelly had disclosed her sexuality to some family and friends, but, to her, the meaning of coming out was purely a matter of self-acceptance and self-affirmation.

Coming out to Family/Friends

Among all of the various meanings participants attributed to coming out, coming out to family/friends was the most common. However, there is definitely variation in what "family" or "friends" means from person to person. For one participant, Brian, family refers specifically to his parents, while for another participant, Carly, the discussion focused more broadly on those people closest to her. Although coming out to family/friends was a highly prevalent theme across the interviews, relatively few participants cited it as the lone element in their meaning of coming out. But, there were a few exceptions—three to be exact: Ari, Nathan, and Adam. This study opened with a quote from Ari, a 28 year-old who identifies as a lesbian. As Ari put it,

The way I define coming out is coming out to my parents because everyone I met and talked to, you know, my colleagues, my professors, my friends, they all knew I was queer, but my parents never knew.

After reflecting on this statement, Ari revisited the meaning of coming out later in the interview. She went on to specify that coming out means more to her than simply telling her parents. "Coming out means telling the people who are closest to you . . . telling the people who matter, and I suppose I'd have to define 'matter' it would be parents, close relatives, close friends." This statement represents a common trend in the meaning of coming out seen throughout this study. The words "family" and "friends" were typically used to refer to those people in one's social network with whom one has high levels of interaction, strong ties, and more meaningful relationships. Extended family and distant friends and acquaintances were rarely spoken about within the context of these conversations, except to point out that coming out to such persons was not central to their meaning of coming out. Those participants who felt that the meaning of coming out includes disclosing their sexuality to extended family and distant peers were also the participants who believed in coming out as "full disclosure"—which will be discussed more below.

Adam, a 20 year-old gay male mirrored Ari's meaning of coming out. Adam discussed broadly how, for him, coming out means disclosing his sexuality to his parents and his close friends. As Adam sees it, the reason that he places so much emphasis on coming out to his parents is because of how long they have known longer him under an assumption of heterosexuality. "No one's going to be harder to come out to than your parents because they had 14 years to get used to the person that they thought they were raising, with the ideals they thought I was going to have, and the future they thought I was going to have." This, he explains, is why family and close friends are central to his meaning of coming out—these relationships are rooted in longer histories, and therefore greater assumptions. Adam talks a great deal about coming out to other people as well—new friends, acquaintances, coworkers—but these interactions are not central to what coming out means to him. Simply put, there is very little at stake with these more distant relationships.

The initial impetus of coming out to my parents, my friends—that was tough. But with every day, every new person I meet it gets a little bit easier, just because I've done it before and I know who I am and who I can depend on, and if it's not the person I'm talking to, that's fine . . .

Much more common was the inclusion of coming out to family/friends as one element in a much broader meaning of coming out. More often than not, coming out to family/friends was combined with coming out to oneself, although it was occasionally paired with coming out as full disclosure. Those participants who spoke about multiple elements to their meaning of coming out rarely referenced any series of fixed "stages" or "steps" that they went through or are going through while coming out. In fact, the only examples of such steps were already shown above in the statements of Brandon and Veronica. Other participants simply saw coming out as having various elements to the meaning, but they never explicitly stated a "formula" for coming out.

Of the participants who spoke about coming out as meaning both coming out to oneself and coming out to family/friends, there was sometimes a hint of time-order in their wording. As stated by Rachel, a 20 year-old female who identifies as gay:

> [Coming out means] coming to terms with who you are and how you feel about who you want to be with, who you want to date, who you feel comfortable with, and who you're attracted to. And, first of all, coming to terms with it yourself and accepting it, and usually telling people you are around and letting them, you know, decide "oh, this is ok with me" . . . I feel like you need to accept yourself before you can let, you know, be able to let others accept you.

Although Rachel iterated a this-before-that causality in her statement, more common was the simple mentioning of both coming out to oneself and coming out to family/friends. Even when causality was not explicitly stated, participants almost always spoke about coming out to oneself before talking about coming out to others. For instance, the meaning of coming out according to Hannah, an 18 year-old female who identifies as gay, is "not just knowing that you're gay or bisexual, but being ok with it, and having the people that are close to you that you want to know—letting them know." Lee, a 20 year-old gay male simplifies the connection even further. Coming out is, "acceptance of yourself, acceptance of your friends knowing who you are." One exception to this implicit or explicit one-way causality was demonstrated by Alex, a 24 year-old female who identifies as gay. "I came out to Pam. That was when I came out to myself. And then it was a half hour of panicking madness." Alex is referencing the first vocal declaration of her sexuality to one of her best friends, Pam. It was not until that moment when she heard herself utter the words out loud that she began to totally accept herself as gay (this is somewhat similar to

Veronica). So, coming out to oneself need not always precede coming out to others.

Whether or not coming out to oneself was achieved prior to coming out to family/friends, one thing is certain: coming out to those within one's social circle is not simply about telling. It is about gaining acceptance, and even more importantly it is about liberation and validation. In fact, the discussion of validation was central to Gabrielle's explanation of why coming out to family/friends was an essential part of her meaning of coming out:

> You come out because you want to be validated, that it's ok. So, it's either coming out to your parents, and them being like "it's ok" or something inside of you and you can't keep it inside yourself because you're too depressed about it but you want to get validated . . . it's a sort of validation, and it's a form of being proud of who you are . . . at the end of the day it's what you feel within yourself, and I think that coming out is a way of getting validated, validating yourself, and encompassing the pride part of it.

The importance of achieving liberation or receiving validation, both from within and from without, was by far strongest among participants who saw coming out to family/friends as central to the meaning of coming out.

In discussing the liberating power of coming out, participants sometimes implied liberation through the use of analogies. Kyle spoke of how coming out "was a huge weight lifted off my shoulders because I had been struggling with that for a while." She was speaking more specifically to the elation she felt after coming out to her mom. Ram, a 21 year-old gay male, spoke about how coming out to his family and friends was an "unburdening." The most colorful analogy came from Alex, who is both a poet and an artist:

> Coming out is owning it, identifying as it, just letting people see it, and even if you are a little bit ashamed of it at first, it's sort of like that good burn, you know, like the first time you go and get a really good, deep-tissue Swedish massage, and the next day you just feel like shit, and the day after it you're like "wow, I feel better now, I can actually move more." So coming out, for me, was like getting a Swedish massage—you can quote me on that.

Other participants that emphasized elation as a result of coming out frequently used singular words like "happy," "free," "open," "honest," "proud," and "real" to describe the feelings that followed coming out to family/friends. I often felt such a positive shift in the interviews upon engaging in this portion of the discussion, which reiterates the centrality of coming out to others in the meaning of coming out for so many people. Of course, for many people the meaning of coming out goes well beyond coming out to family/friends. For about one third of the participants in this study the meaning of coming out can be more aptly described as "full disclosure."

Coming Out as Full Disclosure

> To me (coming out) is just finally being able to be completely yourself in all facets of life. If you're coming out, then you're coming out and you just need to be out. And, I know that's not always the case, and it took me a little bit longer than I wanted it to be. But, I think that eventually when you come out it should be out to everyone.
>
> ~ Renee

For many people, coming out was not limited to the select few family members and friends that make up one's inner circle. Coming out may mean disclosing one's sexuality to any and every one including extended family, casual friends, acquaintances, coworkers, classmates, neighbors, or just people on the street. Much of the conversation surrounding coming out as full disclosure revolves around the idea that to come out means to be yourself in *every* setting, or as Renee put it "to be completely yourself in all facets of life."

Most participants agreed that, given an idyllic setting, they would be out entirely. In fact, some participants flat out stated that they loathe the process, and the social expectations that people with non-heterosexual identities are expected to share their sexualities with others. Brian, a 20 year-old male who identifies as queer emphasized this when discussing the meaning he attributes to coming out. "I think everyone should come out . . . straight people should have to come out as straight, and queer people as queer. I just don't like how it's assumed that everyone is straight—everyone's one way." But, in spite of the current social climate regarding sexuality Brian still maintains that coming out means publicly disclosing one's sexuality broadly to whomever is interested in knowing.

Part of the ideology behind full disclosure is the notion that "if someone doesn't accept me for me, then I don't want to be associated with them anyway." As Veronica explained, "I definitely have always had the tendency to always let people know, almost as soon as possible, that I cannot just waste my time with them if they're gonna reject that part of me." She goes on to state that coming out means full disclosure preceded by coming out to oneself.

> [Coming out means] all the way out, to the fullest extent. Not like "I'm thinking about it" or "I'm curious." It's like "you know, I'm gay, I identify as gay" . . . letting them know. To me, that's "out," but I think there definitely is a two-step process, and I think the most difficult for me was definitely coming out to myself.

The one caveat to the idea that coming out means full disclosure is that an individual may choose to come out entirely within a particular social arena (e.g., an LGBTQ organization in town), yet refrain from coming out in other social arenas (e.g., one's family, close friends, or workplace). The most frequent example of this in my interviews involved those who were disinterested in or unable to come out in the workplace. In discussing how coming out means full disclosure, Gabrielle stated "I'm very proud, so I don't think I would put a level on [how open she is about her sexuality] unless I'm working and that's a different situation." Because of the lack of sexual orientation-based employment protections in her home state, Gabrielle, who is as "out" as can be, is forced to place a figurative asterisk on her "full disclosure."

Since sexual orientation is not a protected class under employment law in many states, participants cited the need to keep their sexualities private in the workplace, regardless of what coming out means to them. Although employment restrictions may curb individuals' degree of outness in the workplace, they did not seem to alter individuals' meanings of coming out. Participants who saw coming out as full disclosure yet were unable to come out at work still maintained that full disclosure was their social goal and the meaning they attribute to coming out nonetheless. The meaning remains unchanged, regardless of the structural barriers that currently prevents one from being as out as one wishes.

The most extreme example of a barrier to full disclosure was seen in my interview with Michelle, a 25 year-old female who identifies as gay. Michelle has spent the past few years employed in the U.S. Armed Services, and still serves actively in the military. To Michelle coming out means full disclosure, but due to her military career she is structurally unable to engage in full disclosure within all social arenas. At the time of our interview, the military was still enforcing Don't Ask Don't Tell, so her desire to engage in full disclosure was limited by her desire to keep her career intact. To a lesser degree, this same situation arose in various other interviews, and the exception always revolved around employment. It would be interesting to ascertain if this same interaction would arise for LGBQ persons residing in states that offered sound legal protections on the basis of sexual orientation.

Still, some participants maintained that coming out literally means true, *full* disclosure. Eden expressed perhaps the most open meaning of coming out as full disclosure, which is reinforced by her personal mantra of living life "openly and honestly."

> [Coming out] means if your family, friends, pets, neighbors, people walking down the street, people on the bus, anybody asks you a question that involves a statement about your sexual identity, orientation, gender identity and expression, then you would divulge. To me coming out means everywhere I go someone's going to hear about it if it comes up in conversation.

Arielle, a 24 year-old who identifies as a lesbian, mirrored the sentiment that full disclosure is in fact *full* disclosure preceded by self-affirmation. To her coming out means gaining self-acceptance of her sexual orientation and "sharing it with everyone regardless of repercussions, whether positive or negative." But many participants, such as Eden and Arielle, recognize that the meaning they personally ascribe to coming out may not necessarily be congruent with the meanings held by other people. Coming out is a very personal experience that depends on a number of social factors, so the meaning of coming out varies substantially.

Discussion and Conclusion

Coming out is an important element in the lives of LGBQ persons, and it is widely considered to be a crucial element in the development of a healthy sexual identity among members of the LGBQ community. It may serve a multitude of functions, not the least of which is self-affirmation and the public disclosure of a non-heterosexual identity. As this study demonstrates, coming out is anything but formulaic—indeed, experiences with coming out are hardly the same from one person to the next. The high degree of variability in coming out is evident in the different meanings participants attributed to the concept itself.

The meaning of coming out varies on the basis of one's life circumstances, social environments, and personal beliefs and values. A singular meaning of coming out cannot be derived without ignoring the broad variation seen across the participants in this study. All 30 participants did agree on one thing: coming out is a transformative, ongoing process—a career. For some participants this transformation was more a personal journey of self-affirmation. Still, for most participants, coming out means much more than just "coming out to oneself." For most participants coming out means (at least in part) the sharing of their sexuality with others. This includes disclosing their sexuality to family and close friends, or perhaps even disclosing their sexuality to any and every one (i.e. full disclosure). Participants most commonly referenced both coming out to oneself and coming out to others as being central to the meaning of coming out.

Aside from detailing the variety of meanings associated with coming out, the single most important contribution of the current study is the finding that coming out is still a relevant concept related to sexual identity formation and maintenance. Seidman et al. (1999), as well as other contemporary sexuality scholars, contend that coming out is no longer focused on legitimating sexualities via an outward disclosure. True enough, for two participants in this study coming out was only about self-affirmation—and not about disclosure at all. Still, coming out was important to them and their sexualities. Evidence from my interviews challenges the notion that coming out is a thing of the past. Every single participant in the current study actively engaged in coming out, and they each considered coming out to be central to their life trajectories.

Coming out is both a personal and a social process that appears to be omnipresent so long as we operate within a heteronormative society. The face of coming out may be changing—many teens and young adults are assumed gay by family and friends (see Chapter 5). The assumption that someone is gay is typically based on outward characteristics that are stereotypically associated with gay culture or a gender presentation based in gender non-conformity (e.g., a masculine female). But, even those who are assumed to be gay still engage in some form of coming out. Consider a teenage girl who is assumed gay, yet confronted by her best friend about her sexuality nonetheless: she will still be faced with matters of self-affirmation and potentially a confirmatory disclosure to her friend—both of which are examples of coming out. Even if her sexuality never becomes a public matter, she will still manage the course of coming out to herself, and she will engage in a career of privatizing the details of her intimate relationships in a manner in which most people in society totally take for granted. Lack of broad public acceptance of one's sexuality lends itself to the compartmentalization of one's personal and social spheres, thus making coming out an enduring, albeit increasingly more familiar and manageable career. The notion that coming out is a career rather than a mere process is the subject of discussion in Chapter 6.

Most researchers that study coming out refer to coming out as a purely external endeavor. An overstated focus on the visible elements of coming out—that is the public disclosure of a sexual identity—can skew the achievement of a full understanding of the concept of coming out. Public media and the heterosexual majority often frame coming out as entirely a matter of "outing" oneself to others (or being outed). But, presuming such a thing limits the scope of research and common understanding of coming out. Kitsuse (1980) warns against conceiving of coming out as only a matter of secrecy and disclosure in his research on deviance. Although Kitsuse is speaking of "coming out" as it relates more broadly to anyone defined by another person as a deviant, his point resonates with the current study. His contention is that, in order to study coming out, special attention must be granted to "the issue of the social affirmation of self" (Kitsuse 1980:1). Coming out is not simply about satisfying the moral majority. Rather, coming out serves as a way to challenge social conventions and expert opinions, and affirm a positive sense of self.

Plenty of people engage in self-acceptance and affirmation yet have no interest in disclosing their sexuality to other people. The finding from this study that, for some people, the meaning of coming out is *entirely* a matter of self-affirmation challenges the meanings utilized by many scholars in which coming out is defined solely as an external endeavor. Further, the realization that coming out can be a purely internal course of action problematizes research that assumes a heterocentric model of coming out focused entirely on explaining difference to others. Many study participants engaged in conversation about whether or not they felt a disclosure imperative was placed upon them by society. Most everyone agreed that we, as a society, expect difference to be explained. But, not everyone shared this sentiment. Some participants felt an expectation to remain closeted, to allow society to delude itself into believing that everyone is straight. Regardless of whether they felt pressured to disclose or explain their difference, most participants agreed that coming out was more than just external.

Considering the frequency with which participants spoke of coming out to oneself as being central to the meaning of coming out, "coming out" should be conceptualized as a social phenomenon that includes—perhaps wholly, but at least partially—self-affirmation (i.e. coming out to oneself). Self-affirmation, then, is not a prerequisite, or even a co-requisite to coming out—self-affirmation *is* coming out. Utilizing a modified definition of coming out that includes self-affirmation, we find that many "closeted" LGBQ individuals are actually engaged in coming out—albeit not outwardly. Regardless of whether or not individuals choose to disclose their sexualities, unless they refuse to personally accept or affirm an LGBQ identity, they are coming out.

In most situations self-affirmation precedes any outward disclosure of one's sexuality. But this is not always the case. Prior to or during self-affirmation people may be "outed" publicly by other people. In such cases, self-affirmation may be the final element in initially coming out rather than the precursor to everything else. And, as seen in our discussion of Veronica above, sometimes the sharing of one's sexuality eases the self-affirmation process by making the whole thing feel more real. In Veronica's case, it was not until she came out to her friend Matty that she earnestly came to affirm her newfound lesbian identity. For many participants self-affirmation and the outward disclosure of a sexual identity were mutually contributory processes.

Participants who are further removed from conventional dualistic thinking (i.e., they think beyond a gender binary) are more inclined to deemphasize coming out to family and friends and focus instead on coming out as a personal journey of self-affirmation. Younger cohorts (roughly born from 1988 forward) appear to be identifying with more *open* sexual identities such as pansexual, queer, and fluid. As these sexualities continue to emerge, we will likely see the meaning of coming out continue to evolve as well. We know very little about coming out among people who identify as pansexual or fluid, but research on bisexuality may provide a clue. People who identify as bisexual, when compared to those who identify as gay or lesbian, are less likely to come out to others (Weinberg et al. 1994; McLean 2007). According to these and other studies of bisexuality, coming out is less central to identity formation for bisexuals. Still, researchers often make this assertion under the assumption that coming out is synonymous with outward disclosure. With the understanding that coming out is both an internal and external endeavor, we see that coming out is still an important— albeit mostly internal—aspect to affirming a healthy bisexual identity.

Part of the difficulty associated with disclosing a bisexual identity is that few people in the general population understand anything about bisexuality (Bradford 2004). As newly emerging sexual identities, pansexuality and fluidity are generally even less understood than bisexuality. Even among the participants in this study, many people were unfamiliar with pansexuality. The lack of public understanding over newly emerging identities may explain why the meaning of coming out among people who identify as pansexual, queer, or fluid, is more about self-affirmation than anything else. Chapter 4 will engage in a discussion of why people who identify as pansexual or fluid oftentimes come out initially as bisexual purely out of fear that their true sexual identity will not be understood by other people. Perhaps in the coming years we will see an increase in the volume of people who perceive of coming out as a purely personal journey. Or perhaps as these newly emerging identities gain exposure, people who identify as pansexual or fluid will in turn place greater importance on the outward sharing of their sexuality.

Despite the handful of participants who stated that coming out was entirely about self-affirmation, the meaning of coming out held by most participants still includes some element of coming out to others. There appears to be a fairly even split between those who emphasize coming out to family/friends versus those who emphasize coming out to any and every one (i.e. coming out as "full disclosure"). As was the case with coming out to oneself, those who stress coming out as being a matter of full disclosure are oftentimes individuals who maintain fluid or open sexualities. But this is not always the case. Many gay and lesbian participants also emphasized full disclosure as a central element in the meaning they attribute to coming out. A few participants who are currently not even interested in "full disclosure" recalled moments early in their coming out trajectories when they were—at least situationally—interested in coming out to everyone. They may not have been shouting out their sexuality to each passerby, but they were more inclined to present themselves as gay lifestylers—what Brekhus (2003) calls "peacocks." A peacock does everything "as a gay person," and consequently engages in coming out nonverbally on a broad scale (Chapter 5 includes a discussion of how some LGBQ persons utilize gender non-conformity as a means of coming out nonverbally). It may be that, as non-heterosexual identities continue to gain broad public acceptance, coming out will be more about full disclosure since individuals will have less to fear about with whom to share their sexuality. Sexuality will become just another part of our overall identities. Then again, as posited by Seidman et al (1999) increased normalization of all sexualities may simply make the public disclosure of one's sexuality unnecessary. Follow-up interviews with the participants in this study may shed some light on the effect of increased public acceptance on coming out.

Considering the degree to which sexual minorities continue to be systematically oppressed, it is difficult to envision coming out as becoming entirely obsolete. Given the current social and political climate, LGBQ persons are still treated as second-class citizens. As long as heterosexuality is viewed as normative, LGBQ persons will continue to engage, at the very least, in self-affirmation—which, according to some people *is* coming out. Even the participants in this study who were raised in the most LGBQ affirming environments found themselves grappling with the idea of being different or letting go of "normality." Despite the best efforts of parents, educators, and religious leaders who wish to foster inclusive environments for children, dominant messages within broad social institutions (lack of marriage equality, lack of benefits for same-sex partners, high rates of bullying) may ring too loud for the individual voices of inclusiveness to be heard.

A few comments should be made about how issues with sampling could influence the findings of this study that relate to the meaning of coming out. One of the biggest challenges with any qualitative study is obtaining a diverse sample. This difficulty is magnified when the study involves a "hidden" population such as sexual minorities. Although, like many other studies on coming out, I had a hard time obtaining racial diversity in the sample, the most challenging characteristic upon which to draw diversity is what I would call the "degree of outness." LGBQ persons who *have* engaged in coming out are well represented in literature on coming out. Conversely, few studies include samples of people who have *not* engaged in any (outward) coming out. If a researcher does an effective job of marketing a study to a broad audience, there is a slim possibility that a participant could emerge who has not disclosed their sexuality to others. Since I relied primarily on snowball sampling, the best I could hope for is locating people who have only disclosed their sexuality to one or two other people. Subsequently, very few of my participants have disclosed their sexuality to only one or two people. The meaning and related experiences of coming out are likely very different amongst those who have are newly engaged in coming out. So I have to recognize this as a limitation of the study. Although there are a few other limitations to the current study (small sample size, lack of participants who identify as black or presently identify as bisexual), the findings and subsequent implications far outweigh the limitations.

The overall issue of *meaning* presents a methodological concern for studying coming out, and any other social phenomena for that matter. As evidenced in this study, individuals attach a variety of meanings to coming out, and these meanings vary based on individual lived experiences. Future research on coming out should take into account the variety of meanings attached to coming out when designing studies—or at least recognize the limitations of using a finite definition of the concept. An assumption of shared meaning should not be made without considering the disparate impact such a practice will have on the outcome of a given study. This last statement is especially valid considering how virtually every study on coming out is centered on it being an external endeavor. This conceptualization of the concept of coming out would serve as a major barrier to learning about coming out among individuals who consider coming out to be wholly (at least partially) a matter of self-affirmation. At the very least, researchers should share their meaning of coming out with participants so that study participants can understand the researcher's position on the concept and therefore provide more meaningful, valid responses to questions. Otherwise the disconnect between researchers' intent with and participants' understanding of a concept may lead to biased findings. After all, research findings are typically analyzed and written up based on the researcher's conceptualization or operationalization of the phenomena under scrutiny—not the participants.

Some sexuality scholars contend that we are moving beyond the closet, and that coming out may no longer serve as a concept relevant to sexual identity formation and maintenance. Although many young people today are not growing up in the closet, figuratively speaking, the maintenance of a non-heterosexual identity still requires individuals to engage in coming out. Even those individuals who are "assumed gay" based on their gender presentation sometimes find themselves engaged in coming out—if nothing else, simply to affirm someone else's suspicions. As one of the participants in this study, Nathan, pointed out, the disclosure of an LGBQ identity is oftentimes not even done verbally. People utilize their physical presentation and dress in order to communicate difference, and therefore come out. It does seem to be true that the dynamics of coming out are changing. Less often are youth engaging in storytold interactions where they come out collectively to their entire families. Coming out occurs much more casually, and it is often handled situationally with singular friends, family members, or peers. Although it may be less about monumental moments, coming out is still an influential part of the life trajectory for many, if not most LGBQ persons.

---

[1] An earlier version of this chapter appears in a 2013 journal article entitled "The Meaning of Coming Out: From Self-affirmation to Full Disclosure" published in *Qualitative Sociology Review* (Volume 9, Issue 2).

3

The Use of Bisexuality as a Transitional Identity

I just came out with it to Matty. I was like, "oh, you know, I'm bisexual," because most people, when they come out . . . I mean most of the people that I've met, or many, not most, many, coming out as bisexual first I found is very common.

~Veronica

Veronica has never been attracted to men, but she came out initially as bisexual nonetheless. She does recognize that many men and women fall along a Kinsey-esque continuum, but she refers to herself as "a very rare case of really strong preference to women." She is fully aware that society expects her to be attracted to men, so much so that she tried dating boys throughout her youth—boys for which she "couldn't muster feelings or sexual attraction" whatsoever. As she stated emphatically, "I shouldn't have to try this hard, and fail every time, you know, to muster any kind of romantic or sexual feelings for the opposite sex." Incidentally, she eventually accepted the fact that she is only attracted to women and she came out as a lesbian. Veronica's decision to come out initially as bisexual may appear to be nothing more than an idiosyncratic characteristic of her own trajectory of coming out. But the reality is that she is highlighting a broader social trend—a new dynamic of coming out.[1]

Outside of heterosexuality, the most prevalent sexuality in the United States is bisexuality (Gates 2011). Students in my sexuality courses are always baffled to learn that more Americans identify with bisexuality than homosexuality—a collective reaction which is based largely in the relative invisibility of bisexuality. Despite the prevalence of bisexuality in the U.S., it is still largely marginalized within the

LGBTQ community (Ochs 1996). People who maintain bisexual identities are continually pressured to identify as either gay or straight, and these demands are particularly strong within the LGBTQ community (Rust 2000). It seems plausible then that the use of bisexuality as a transitional identity may help explain the marginalization of bisexuality, and the refusal among many people to treat it as an authentic identity in its own right. The use of bisexuality as a transitional identity, as Veronica asserts, is quite common, and it is largely the result of heteronormative social forces.

Heterosexuals rarely, if ever, have to justify the characteristics of their dominant sexuality. In the U.S., privilege is held by those who are white, male, and—of import to this study—heterosexual. In our society heterosexuality is framed as "normal." Research even suggests that heterosexuals do not typically consider their sexual orientation as a defining element in their self-identity (Diamond 2008). It is simply not thought about. When a characteristic is normative it is rarely called into question. The notion that heterosexuality is "normal," "typical," and "ideal" is echoed throughout U.S. institutions ranging from schools and churches to legal guidelines to the mass media. Additionally, participants in the current study spoke frequently of the heteronormative expectations placed upon them by their families, their friends, their teachers, and other authority figures. Considering all of these social forces, it is not surprising to see that many youth grapple with whether or not to affirm an LGBQ identity or come out at all. But what about those individuals who do affirm an LGBQ identity?

An extensive body of literature exists regarding why an individual may choose *not* to come out. Studies often cite the influence of family and friends, social norms, or even refusal on the part of the individual to affirm an LGBQ identity (Jordan and Deluty 1998; Waldner and Magruder 1999; Merighi and Grimes 2000; Appleby 2001; Flowers and Buston 2001; Johnston and Jenkins 2003; McLean 2007; Gorman-Murray 2008). However, rarely does research focus on the details of how these same three social influences alter the way in which an individual *does* come out. Rather than preventing someone from even engaging in coming out, these powerful forces can influence someone to come out in a compromised fashion. That is, individuals may come out with an identity that differs from their internalized sexuality in an effort to be more palatable to all parties involved in coming out (family, friends, even oneself). I call this interaction the *queer apologetic*.

The Queer Apologetic

From a very young age, people are bombarded with a multitude of messages concerning the heteronormative expectations of our society. Family is often cited as one of the first—and consequently most influential—sources of heteronormative expectations. Most people who are born into two-parent households are brought up by a woman and a man, a mother and a father (such was the case for 22 of the 30 participants in this study). Of these 22 people, 18 reported having intact families consisting of a biological mother and father who are still together, and another four grew up with mom and dad who are now separated. Heteronormative social messages originating in sources as broad as Disney movies and U.S. state laws reiterate the expectation that "man + woman = normal." These messages are highly influential, and they serve as constant reminders of what is expected of people in their future relationships. Heterosexuality is normative, so much so that queer youth often go to great lengths to hold onto it. As Diamond (2008:58) aptly suggests, "the presumption of universal heterosexuality is so strong that [many women] never have to question it." This presumption is what makes coming out such an arduous journey for many ·LGBQ persons.

Members of the LGBQ community are well aware that their sexuality is not the norm, and that their status as a sexual minority makes life more challenging in many ways. You may recall a poignant quote from Chapter 1 in which Gabrielle, a 22 year-old who identifies as a lesbian, recalls some of the media and cultural forces that continued to push her toward heterosexuality as a young girl.

> When I was little all I could think about was me under a fucking hopa [a Jewish altar], getting married and the guy stepping on the fucking glass, and having an awesome crazy-big wedding because I'm very big like that, and that's all I could think about . . . you think about your wedding day as a little girl . . . And, playing Barbie . . . Barbie and Ken, you make them fuck, you don't make the two . . . well, maybe you do make the two girls fuck, but you know what I mean. That's always how it's been and the all of the sudden you either meet people who are like this, or you are just realizing or you find that you have this attraction toward this person or that person, and you just don't understand why and it's something that's deep inside of you.

Throughout the interviews in this study, participants frequently spoke of experiences similar to those in Gabrielle's recollection. Individuals spoke most often of expectations placed upon them by their parents, themselves, and society in general. Such heavy social expectations often force individuals to grapple with their sexuality much more than should be expected given that sexuality is often purported to be a very personal matter The desire to satisfy social expectations, please other people, and be comfortable with oneself can therefore lead an individual to disclose a sexual identity that does not truly match one's inner feelings of sexuality. This interaction, termed the *queer apologetic*, is an original phrase used to describe a phenomenon that is well known anecdotally, but until now has been unnamed academically. The queer apologetic is a significant addition to the literature. It provides an empirical explanation for the decision by many queer individuals to engage in identity compromises during the formation and maintenance of their sexual identities.

The queer apologetic is an individual's attempt at minimizing disapproval of and disappointment over her sexuality by disclosing a public identity that she feels will be more easily accepted by family/friends or even herself. The queer apologetic is essentially a form of identity compromise whereby individuals locate and disclose an intermediate or transitional identity situated somewhere between a) their personal attractions for only members of the same sex and b) society's expectation that they be attracted only to members of the other sex. Such circumstances were discussed by 10 of the 30 participants in the current study, highlighting that this process is far more than an anomaly. Despite their interest in and attraction to *only* members of the same sex, many participants spoke about coming out publicly as bisexual.

Previous literature on other "apologetics" refer to strategies for bridging the gap between cultural expectations and the perception that one's situation (i.e., coming out) challenges those expectations. Rohrbaugh (1979) spoke of such apologetics being employed by female athletes who were aware of the contested (male dominated) terrain within which they were operating. Most research on the apologetic surrounds certain social institutions—namely politics, sports, and religion (Benoit 1995)—but the concept of the apologetic applies to other domains in which individuals encounter a problematic situation (such as a violation of social expectations regarding sexuality).

As Goffman (1971) points out, one of the primary motivations for individuals to engage in apologetic interactions is to maintain healthy relationships with valued people (family, friends, etc.). And although the queer apologetic is intended to ease the process of coming out, the apologetic nature of the exchange actually works to reinforce existing arrangements regarding sexuality. Apologetic interchanges may be short, but they are often campaigns that are developed over time (Benoit

1995). This last characteristic of apologetic interchanges was echoed throughout my interview data, as many participants navigated their queer apologetic for months, even years.

A final point is that the concept of the queer apologetic is not necessarily about offering an apology for one's non-heterosexual orientation. It has much to do with expressing regret for the occurrence of an undesirable event (Schlenker and Darby 1981). An example of this distinction can be seen in the gay theology movement of the 1950s— which was also largely apologetic (Krondorfer 2007). Individuals who were involved in the movement were not so much apologizing for their sexuality; rather, they were apologetic about the situation caused by their movement (based on their acknowledgement of a mainstream belief that gay Christians represented a paradox of sorts). It is the difference between saying "I'm sorry that I'm gay" and saying "I'm sorry that my being gay has raised an issue that is difficult for the church to deal with."

The ten participants in this study who engaged in a queer apologetic were (and still are) attracted only to members of the same sex, so their initial disclosure of a bisexual identity was an apologetic endeavor. It was apologetic in that the compromised identity was put forth purely for people whom the individuals perceived would be less able or willing to accept a gay identity (which may have included themselves). The interesting element of these individuals' experiences is that they came out as bisexual either for the sake of their family/friends or because they were personally not ready to let go of social conventions. So, in the eyes of individuals who are coming out, the disclosure of a bisexual identity allowed them to express their interest in members of the same sex while still allowing others (and sometimes themselves) to hold out hope that an eventual partner of the other sex could be secured. At least that was the intent and their belief at the onset of first coming out.

To their surprise, their identity compromise backfired in nearly every circumstance. Although participants may have felt like they were coming out with a sexual identity that satisfied both themselves and others, they later came to realize that our society's reliance on heavily dualistic thinking derided their progress. In the eyes of many Americans, and consequently the friends and family of many of my participants, bisexuality involves (at least partially) "liking members of the same sex" and this is seen as synonymous with being gay (Lindley et al. 2012). People judge and label others based on what they see, and since bisexuality is not outwardly visible in a single moment a bisexual person is typically assumed to be either gay or straight—depending upon the sex of their current partner (Rust 2000). Consistent with current research on sexual identities, intermediate identities (a concept itself rooted in faulty dualistic thinking) that fall somewhere in between heterosexuality and homosexuality are less understood and therefore not as easily explained or accepted (Eliason 1996; Lucal 2008). As such, rather than accepting or affirming the newly disclosed bisexual identity, family members and friends resoundingly pushed for the individual to "choose a side" or "admit that you're gay." In this way, the decision to come out initially with a bisexual identity made for a much more difficult route to disclosing an internalized sexuality which eventually aligned with a gay or lesbian identity.

The concept of the queer apologetic focuses on individuals' usage of bisexuality as a transitional identity. This same interaction was documented by Rosario et al (2006) in their longitudinal study of 156 LGB youth. Among their sample, 18 percent of participants came out initially as bisexual but later affirmed a gay or lesbian identity. Despite the prevalence of this pattern, bisexuality is by no means purely a transitional identity. An absolute number of bisexual persons is difficult to determine in that bisexuality is masked in invisibility (See and Hunt 2011). However, Burleson (2005) estimates that there are at least 5 million bisexual people in the United States. Of the 30 individuals in this study, bisexuality served as the *initial* public sexual identity for 15 total participants (10 of which engaged in a queer apologetic). Although nobody in the current study presently identifies as bisexual, one participant, Hannah, does recall having initially come out as bisexual based on her sincere attractions to both men and women.

> [I told] my parents that I was bisexual, and they had thought it was a phase, which really for some reason, really upset me, and because I was so sure of it and I was like "no, I definitely like both." I was positive I was bisexual for a long time. I was 100% . . . I was like "I like both and I will always like both."

Hannah has since affirmed a gay identity. As she put it "I started dating women and I hit 9th grade of high school, and I realized 'I'm gay, I'm gay.'" Still, Hannah represents the only participant in this study who initially came out as bisexual, identifies presently as gay or lesbian, and did *not* engage in a queer apologetic. She had mutual attractions for men and women at the time, so her disclosure of a bisexual identity was not apologetic.

The 15 individuals in this study who previously disclosed a bisexual identity all presently identify as gay, lesbian, queer, pansexual, or they simply choose not to identify. The present analysis of the queer apologetic applies solely to those 10 individuals who were interested only in members of the other sex (all of whom eventually affirmed a gay or lesbian identity). The other 5 individuals who initially came out as bisexual have since affirmed a different sexual identity, but these individuals are all sincerely interested in dating multiple genders or they simply do not use gender as criteria for choosing intimate partners. Therefore, they did not engage in a queer apologetic—there was no compromise. Their decision to come out as bisexual was rooted in the perception that other people would likely not understand what it means to be pansexual, queer, etc. But, for the 10 participants who presently identify as gay or lesbian, their journey through bisexuality was truly apologetic.

Pleasing Family/Friends

In contemporary society, it is still often expected that anyone who is not explicitly heterosexual should "explain their difference." It seems safe to assume that when someone does disclose a lesbian, gay, bisexual, or queer identity, it means that she does, in fact, privately identify as such. But considering what we know about the effects of heteronormativity on coming out, it should come as no surprise to learn that public identities and private sexualities do not always align. Just as someone who privately identifies as gay may remain closeted, another individual who privately identifies as gay may come out publicly as bisexual.

Just as social science research is often filled with people's attempts at providing socially desirable responses to survey questionnaires (Groves et al. 2009), people sometimes present a public identity that they believe to be more palatable to their audience—and sexual orientation is no exception. In the case of sexual identity disclosure, that audience typically consists of family and close friends. People care deeply about being accepted or even validated by family and friends. Fear of rejection is a powerful force, especially when it involves those people we rely on most. Even children and teens worry about how their coming out will be received regardless of whether or not they have close relationships with their families. Research suggests that those with healthy families have an even greater fear of rejection than those who have weak family ties (Waldner and Magruder 1999). LGBQ persons who come from unsupportive homes have more dire reasons to worry (e.g., direct threats from family members or outwardly homophobic dialog in the home), but in many ways there is more to lose in the case of healthy, happy families. Considering the high percentage of close-knit, intact families in this study, it makes sense that fear of rejection would prove instrumental in guiding the trajectory of coming out for most of the participants.

Aside from pure fear, participants also indicated a strong desire to simply please their families. Just as people often try to make their parents proud by performing well in school or landing a good job, many participants chose to disclose a sexual identity that they believed would meet their parents' expectations of sexuality—at least partially. Most parents raise their children under the assumption that their children are heterosexual. In extreme cases, such parental expectations may keep an individual from coming out at all, opting instead for the maintenance of a publicly heterosexual identity, at least around the family. Hamed, a 30 year-old gay male, was not comfortable speaking at length about his coming out, but he did offer some poignant insight on living under an assumption of heterosexuality at home:

> My friends, everyone at school, they knew I was gay . . . I never really made a point of keeping that part of myself private. I even came out to my parents at one point, but they just sent me to a therapist who was supposed to cure me, and even now, as far as my parents know, I am "cured" . . . when I'm at home with family I am heterosexual.

However, for most participants, hiding or denying all same-sex attractions was simply not an option. Some participants spoke specifically about how much of an imperative it was to come out. As Gabrielle put it, "regardless if I was being paid a million dollars, I would not want to be in the closet." The decision to keep one's sexuality entirely private would require the compartmentalization of one's entire life into separate social spheres. Such was the case for Michelle, a 25 year-old gay woman, who is reluctantly closeted in certain social circles due to her military service: "Well, I can only come out sometimes. Obviously, with the military you're not supposed to [come out]." At the time of our interview, Don't Ask Don't Tell was still being enforced. A much more feasible choice undertaken by many participants was to opt instead for the disclosure of a public sexual identity that would both 1) allow them to maintain their own interest in same-sex relations, and 2) uphold the other-sex expectations of their family/friends. Enter: bisexuality.

The queer apologetic is an individual's attempt at minimizing disapproval of and disappointment over her true sexual identity by disclosing a public identity *believed to be* more palatable to her family/friends or herself. I emphasize the words "believed to be" because an individual's perception of how her family and friends will react often fails to match up with reality. But, the *perception* that family and friends would be more likely to accept a bisexual identity than a gay or lesbian identity is prevalent across many participants. One of the clearest examples of such thinking was demonstrated by Rachel, a 20 year-old woman who presently identifies as gay.

> I couldn't stop getting thoughts out of my head about just women, and like, just being gay. And so that's when I kind of cracked, and I told someone because he had told me . . . he had come out to me as gay and he told me I was the only person that he told, and so I felt comfortable with him and I just kind of told him and from there it was a snowball effect . . . Um, telling my mom . . . at first though I told them that I was bisexual because I thought that they'd be more accepting, but in reality I was just trying to ease them into it.

Rachel was slowly getting comfortable with the reality that she only "liked women," but she still felt inclined to come out to her mom as bisexual. She envisioned bisexuality as a sort of go-between or a compromise between her interest in only members of the same sex and her perception that her mom wished to see her date members of the other sex. So, despite her honest lack of interest in "guys," she came out as bisexual.

> I told [her mother] that I like girls, and I said that maybe I'm bi-, just to make it easier . . . and so she kept questioning me, "well, what do you think you are?" [Reflecting back] I just tried to convince myself "ok, I'm bi-. I'm just going to be bi-." Like, I told myself, "I can be bi- if I want to. I like girls but I can try to like guys,"—which wasn't the case.

She inferred from this conversation that her mom was pressuring her to say that she might still be interested in guys. But, it was actually quite the opposite. Her mom was not concerned about the sex or gender of her daughter's romantic interests—she was merely set on her daughter being either explicitly gay or explicitly heterosexual. The decision to engage in an identity compromise seemed, at least initially, to backfire and make the entire coming out process more difficult. Her mom questioned and pressured her to affirm a gay identity.

> My mom said, "Rachel, I think you're gay, and you need to be able to accept that," and so she was kind of like, not arguing with me, but really stern about it like "you really need to be ok with it, and it's great that you came out, but if you're gay you're gay," so . . .

Rachel's expectation that other people would be more affirming of a bisexual identity was not limited to her parents. Even among her group of close friends, she anticipated that they would be more likely to accept her coming out with an identity that left the door open for dating men. But, her decision to come out as bisexual was more about pleasing other people than trying to make her own coming out less difficult. Her actions really seemed to communicate an apologetic response to the realization that she was only attracted to members of the same sex.

> In high school I [came out as bisexual], just because I thought they'd accept me more if they're like "ok, well, maybe she'll like a guy again," I mean I felt like it was just a way to ease people into it [the fact that she privately identified as gay]. At first I just said "I like girls," and they just assumed that I was bi- because I had dated all these guys that they knew . . . I just wanted to please everyone, and try to make it easier for them.

Now that Rachel has moved beyond trying to anticipate what her family and friends would prefer to see her identify as, she is comfortable outwardly admitting that, "I have no interest in being with men . . . I definitely consider myself gay, I'm a lesbian, I just don't like the term, so I'll call myself gay." So, in Rachel's case, the only force that encouraged her to engage in a queer apologetic was her perception that family and friends would be more likely to affirm an identity that still had a partial foothold in heterosexuality. Although she only indicated feeling pressured by the perceived expectations of family and friends, the fact that there was such a big disconnect between perception and reality also uncovers the power of cultural ideology. She had built up the notion that being accepted was contingent upon appearing to have at least some level of interest in men.

Another example of the level of influence that family can have on the public disclosure of a sexual identity can be seen in the experiences of Kyle, a 21 year-old who presently identifies as a lesbian. Throughout her interview, Kyle expressed that she has never liked boys/men. She laughingly recalls "dating" a male friend in high school (whom she knew to be gay) purely to see what her friends' reactions would be and during the process she realized "man, I am sooo gay, and he's sooo gay, but I was still not telling people." Although she was beginning to come to terms with being attracted only to women, she was nowhere near ready to come out to her family. But, as she recalls, fate had a different plan. One day her mom came across a note that she had written to a girl she was "crushing on" in her class. Her mom "flipped out, describing lesbians [with words like] carpet-muncher . . ." and scaring Kyle into believing that she could never come out as a lesbian.

Based on her conversation with her mom after the note was found, she was more afraid than ever to ever say that she was attracted to women—much less, attracted to *only* women. But, as time progressed, it became increasingly difficult for her to be interested in women yet hide all signs of these interests at home. After a couple of years Kyle became sure that disclosing a bisexual identity was what she wanted to do. It would accomplish 1) conveying to her mom that she "liked girls" while 2) simultaneously allowing her mom to maintain that her child might still end up with a boy.

> And, then, two years later I was like "I think I'm bisexual," and she's like "you better choose a sex," and I'm just like "ok??" [her mannerism communicated a sense of "whatever"] and when I finally came out as a lesbian she was like "that's great honey." And, I was like "for years you made me feel like crap" and she was like "I just wanted you to choose." I'm like "you're insane."

The strain that was created by Kyle having come out as bisexual was severe. At the time that she came out, it seemed to make perfect sense to her that the disclosure of a bisexual identity was the safest bet overall. As was the case with Rachel, it would serve to achieve the goal of expressing that she liked girls while still leaving the door open for future relationships that might involve boys. But, this apologetic identity compromise forced her to take two steps back. For a great deal of time after she came out as bisexual, she and her mom plainly avoided any discussion of attractions or dating whatsoever. When she finally did come out as a lesbian her relationship with both of her parents improved remarkably. She just never would have predicted that her mom would have been more affirming of a lesbian identity than she was a bisexual identity.

> I don't know what she thinks about bisexuals, but she doesn't like them {laughter}. I'm just like "ok, she's comfortable that I'm gay, like, she's fine with that now," but just in the moment she's like "I hate all bisexuals, and my daughter will not be bisexual," and I'm just like [sarcastically] "right on."

Kyle's perception that her parents would be more accepting of a bisexual identity was very influential across the course of her coming out. Most telling is the clear step-wise pattern to her coming out. She first came out to her friends and her sister as "liking girls," then she came out to everyone as bisexual, and finally she came out across the board as a lesbian.

Kyle was not the only participant who came out first as "liking girls" or "liking boys." "Liking girls" is more about expressing an affinity than disclosing an identity, so it was seen initially by many participants as the safest way to come out, especially when an individual had yet to form a concrete sexual identity. As Ari described, "It's not so much me saying 'I'm bisexual,' as much as it is 'do you like girls?' and I respond 'yes.'" Similarly, Rachel "would tell people, you know, that *I like girls*, but I never said 'hey I'm gay,' or 'I'm a lesbian,' so I kind of '*I like girls*,' that's how I kind of brought it up to people (emphasis added)." But the family and friends of most participants insisted on attaching an identity to the individual. In the eyes of many participants, such as Rachel, Kyle, and Ari, bisexuality offered the next best alternative. Of course, their decision to come out as bisexual was based in the assumption that family and friends would be open to someone being attracted to both men and women.

However strong the influence of family and friends may be, it is not the only social force one faces upon deciding to come out. Perhaps the most influential force comes from within. After all, we all have to live with ourselves much more than anyone else has to put up with us. For many participants, letting go of the normative sexual identity (i.e., heterosexuality) felt like an insurmountable challenge. Participants spoke of trying as hard as they could to hold on to social conventions and not let go of "normalcy," despite knowing that they were only interested in relationships with members of the same sex.

Holding on to Social Conventions

Heteronormative expectations—even the subsequent fear of rejection—do not always come from outside sources. One of the most powerful forms of rejection comes from within—via one's own refusal to affirm a non-heterosexual identity (Jordan and Deluty 1998). Heteronormative expectations become such a routinized practice for many people that the first hint of non-heterosexual thoughts or behavior can lead to extreme self-doubt, denial, frustration, confusion, and even all-out self-rejection (Carrion and Lock 1997). As Pao demonstrated:

> It was a process of denial . . . of . . . I think you just go through so many processes to completely, completely, completely come out and accept yourself for who you are. It's just so long, and it's dreadful and it's—you torture yourself a lot and you go through so much before

accepting it. You're taught that it's wrong, so you're fighting against yourself.

The internalized reactions exhibited by participants in this study could only be described as internalized heteronormativity. Literature often speaks of people engaging in internalized homophobia, but participants did not express fear of LGBQ identities, rather they were simply trying to hold onto heteronormative conventions. Internalized heteronormativity was not limited to those who engaged in a queer apologetic—this trend was seen throughout the interviews of most participants. Still, participants engaging in a queer apologetic uniquely spoke of a fear of not conforming to their own heterocentric social expectations. Kelly demonstrated this:

> This girl I was interested in in high school, I kind of got really close to her, and then psyched myself out. I was like "no, no, no, this isn't me," and made up all of these excuses because I was initially scared of what other people might think about me, and, which, usually isn't me at all, so I was really scared by all the new things surrounding it . . . so, I was kind of in denial myself, and then it was kind of a process of me questioning, you know, like "I don't know, do I need to define myself? What is all of this?"

The influence of social conventions and normative heterosexuality was strong among many participants who engaged in a queer apologetic. In fact, three participants, Veronica, Lee, and Pao, placed little to no emphasis on the perceived reactions of family or friends when deciding to come out as bisexual. Their decision to come out initially as bisexual, despite their attractions to only members of the same sex, was rooted entirely in their personal refusal to let go of "normalcy." Admitting that one was gay rather than bisexual or simply someone who "liked girls/boys" would figuratively shut the door on any hope that one would blend into the mass of heterosexual identities seen across contemporary society. This personal, internal struggle is the real differentiation here. Participants who engaged in a queer apologetic rooted in pleasing family were only engaging in the *public* disclosure of a bisexual identity. But, participants whose queer apologetic was based in their personal refusal to let go of social conventions were also deluding *themselves* that they were still interested in members of the other sex. Put more succinctly, the first group engaged in an outward apologetic, while the second group engaged in both an inward and outward apologetic.

The realization that one is "different" (i.e., queer) by social standards can be difficult to digest. Initial reactions range from disbelief to amusement, but the influence of years of messages rooted in heteronormativity leads many people to struggle with the realization that they are attracted to members of the same sex and may, in fact, be gay. This is also oftentimes the point when individuals begin to differentiate between same-sex *affinities* and a more fixed non-heterosexual *identity*. Veronica recalls this very distinction as a point of comfort in her struggle to accept herself. "[Coming out as bisexual] was more for me . . . definitely for me. Um, because my first thought wasn't 'oh, I'm totally gay,' it was just *admitting that I liked girls*" (emphasis added).

Veronica recalls coming out to her good guy-friend Matty as her first real recognition that there existed some internal barriers to affirming a lesbian identity.

> I just came out with it to Matty. I was like, "oh, you know, I'm bisexual," because most people, when they come out . . . I mean most of the people that I've met, or many, not most, many, coming out as bisexual first I found is very common. For me, it was that *holding on to normality* a little bit, and then realizing that, you know, I just don't [like guys] I don't at all . . . and I shouldn't have to try this hard, and fail every time, you know, to muster any kind of romantic or sexual feelings for the opposite sex. But, I was telling . . . I was just like "yeah," and it just came out of my mouth . . . I hadn't planned it (emphasis added).

In Veronica's summation she was already well-aware of her interest in only women, but when it came to the public disclosure of a sexual identity she could not overcome the influence of heteronormative ideology. In that moment she forged an identity compromise which consisted of coming out to her best friend, and consequently herself, as bisexual.

Veronica stated that her decision to come out first as bisexual had nothing to do with the perception that her family or friends would reject a lesbian identity (her present identity), it was a matter of—as she put it—"holding onto normality." Her queer apologetic was directed at satisfying the social expectations of one person—herself. "My family is open-minded, very open-minded . . . [My mom] told me from the very beginning that homosexuality is totally natural . . . None of it was for anybody else, but it was definitely the first step for me." Her disclosure of a bisexual identity was a compromise, but, for Veronica, it was a necessary step in her personal coming out. She soon realized that she was surrounded by a great number of people who were all accepting of gay and lesbian identities, so she began to be self-affirming of a lesbian identity very shortly after coming out as bisexual. "When I was coming out, I realized that I was a lesbian within two weeks of coming out as bisexual . . . I mean it was very quick, the realization." Although she began to self-identify as a lesbian two weeks after coming out as bisexual, it still took a while before she would publicly identify as such. "[It was] like a month and a half before I started coming out [as a lesbian]. Everyone around me was like 'cool, cool, awesome, whatever.' Some of them were like 'duh.'" So, although Veronica faced numerous challenges in disclosing and affirming a lesbian identity, her greatest challenge came from within.

The internalized social conventions of "man + woman = couple" was particularly strong for another participant, Pao, who also engaged in a queer apologetic rooted in holding onto social conventions. Pao provided rich detail as to why she harbored such internalized heteronormativity. For starters, she grew up in Ecuador. Ecuador is, as Pao put it, "a third world country . . . gays and lesbians are like thirty years behind here." She was always attracted to women, as long as she can remember. But she grew up around such intolerance for homosexuality that she recalls, as a child, wishing she was a boy. Girls cannot be with girls, she thought, but if she was a boy then everything would be alright.

> It's only when I think I reached my adolescent stage, like around 18 or 19 . . . way later that I was like "no, I'm a girl and I'm really happy to be a feminine girl." But, it took me awhile to snap out of that [earlier] stage.

It was around this same time that Pao started to be more accepting of the fact that that she "likes girls" and that her attraction to women was not a phase. Still, her inability to let go of social convention—that is, her beliefs and values—kept her from affirming a gay identity (her present identity).

> It wasn't until I was 18. I remember I graduated from high school and I told my best friend. I started because I think, I, I, thought I was bisexual . . . I think that happens to a lot of gay people, they first think they're bisexual and they go through thinking they're bisexual until . . . . and it's just an excuse to accept . . . it's like a pact you take until you truly accept who you are. You say "I like girls but I still like guys," so I started saying I was bisexual.

For Pao bisexuality was a phase until she was able to let go of what she perceived to be semi-heterosexuality and affirm that she is purely interested in members of the same sex. Pao's insistence on disclosing and maintaining a bisexual identity was embedded in her own insistence that she *should* be attracted to men as well as women. "It was a long process because I went through two years of thinking I was bisexual." The internalization of her bisexual identity came to an end just after her first experience with a girl.

> I thought I did [identify as bisexual], I really did think I did, but it wasn't until I had my first experience with a girl. . . when I understood what it was really like to feel attracted to . . . to really like being kissed, and then that, like, shook my world apart.

Pao's internalized apologetic seems easily explainable considering the social environment in which she grew up. However, even those participants who grew up in open, affirming environments were not immune to developing heterocentric ideologies. Lee, a 20 year-old male who now identifies as gay, grappled with his interest in men for years. Despite his resounding lack of interest in women, Lee came out as bisexual. "I tried to say I was bisexual—that's what I said at the time, but I knew at the time that this was me kind of denying it. I guess you don't really notice that until after the fact." Throughout the interview, Lee reiterated that he was only interested in men, and that his decision to come out as bisexual was not a function of trying to please his family or friends. "My family, like my nuclear family, they're pretty affirming." The pressure came from his personal refusal to let go of social conventions.

Lee was convinced of his bisexual identity at the time that he first came out. But, now he is starkly aware of the broad social forces that inundated him with images of heteronormativity and therefore encouraged him to hold onto the social convention of being attracted to members of the other sex. He also presently identifies as gay, and this realization came only after he finally affirmed that he truly is not attracted to women. The most telling statement from Lee's entire interview is actually a surprisingly simple summation of why he now identifies as gay. "I think the only reason that, for me, I stick with gay, is because, as I said before, I haven't been able to become attracted to a girl to the sense where I could have a relationship with her." The power in Lee's admission lies in his wording: "I haven't been able to become . . ." The mere phrasing of this sentence shows just how much social pressure there is to conform to a heteronormative ideal of intimate relationships. The language subtly communicates that, even today, Lee senses that he *should* be attracted to women. It also explains why Lee came out first as bisexual, and then eventually as gay. His admission that he now identifies as gay runs parallel to his newfound realization that he is not "able to become attracted to a girl."

As was the case with Kelly, Veronica, Pao, and Lee, Gabrielle was initially committed to the idea of "holding onto both worlds." Gabrielle is the prototypical example of someone who, despite engaging in coming out, hung onto social conventions throughout much her trajectory. She moved, almost methodically, through a series of transitional labels and identities; each one with slightly less involvement in other-sex attractions.

> I came out as bi-curious, and then I came out as bisexual, and um, my parents are cool with it—I mean, they weren't cool with it—they're cool with it now, but basically, as the years went by I didn't feel comfortable really calling myself a lesbian because I wanted to hold onto both worlds, I guess to feel normal, you know.

Gabrielle came out as 1) liking girls, 2) bi-curious, 3) bisexual, and then finally 4) a lesbian. During none of these phases did she ever earnestly feel attracted to men. Still, in her reflections, she emphasized just how committed she was to hanging onto both worlds. She characterized her movement through the first three periods as "transitional"—slowly easing her into a lesbian identity. Gabrielle's trajectory is reminiscent of "sexual fluidity" as seen in Diamond's (2008) research on women's love and desire. Despite maintaining a fairly congruent internal disposition, she changed identities across time. The queer apologetic provides an explanation for why some individuals move through multiple affinities/identities—that is, it helps explain the apparent sexual fluidity demonstrated by certain individuals.

Tug and Pull: Social Conventions versus Family Influences

Many participants who engaged in an identity compromise via the queer apologetic were influenced purely by their internal desire to conform to social conventions. But other participants whose queer apologetics were based in the internal struggle to hang on social conventions also faced a second, antithetical force in the encouragement of family and friends to identify as either straight or—more often than not—gay. In the cases of three participants, Pao, Gabrielle and Adam, their families' encouragement to identify explicitly as gay or straight actually helped them overcome their own internal bias toward maintaining an identity that allowed for other-sex attraction.

It has already been demonstrated that family and friends often encourage individuals who come out as bisexual to "take a side." Those individuals who engaged in a queer apologetic based in pleasing family or friends were sincerely surprised to find that the people close to them preferred that they identify as gay. These individuals erroneously assumed that other people would be more accepting of an identity that still had at least a partial foothold in heterosexuality. The decision, then, to disclose a bisexual identity turned out to be based on *false perceptions* of what an individual's family or friends would be willing to accept. In the end, family and friends often push the individual to one end of the spectrum. Pao, Gabrielle and Adam all perceived of this "push" as exactly what was needed in order to help them realize that their disinterest in members of the other sex did not mesh with the maintenance of a bisexual identity. For example, in Pao's purview, her sister—who encouraged her to admit that she was not attracted to men—was not forcing her to take a side; rather, she was helping her admit the truth.

> One day my sister called me and I was telling her about this girl, and my sister was like, "you know what?," she told me "Pao, I don't think you like guys. I think you should just be true to yourself—be honest with yourself and if you don't like guys, it's ok," and I was like, "you know what Nati," that's her name, "I actually think you're right, I don't like guys, I like *just* girls," and that was the first time I had admitted it to anybody, which was my sister, which was pretty cool. After that it was like another coming out process—telling everybody I'm not really bisexual.

Gabrielle also cited the influence of family members in helping her affirm a lesbian identity. Although she came out as bisexual based on her own desire to "live in both worlds," internal forces were not the only strain on her sexuality. Her family and friends placed a great deal of pressure on her as well. They continued to push her to choose a side. Although her family was encouraging her to take *a* side, Gabrielle initially interpreted this encouragement as pushing her to take *the* side—of heterosexuality.

> My mom—she's trying to hold onto the fact that there is still a possibility with boys. [I came out to her as] bi-curious, then bisexual, and then eventually my mom was just like "you know, what are you?" I feel like I'm always . . . [her mom pushes her to] "choose Gabrielle, choose what you fucking are." I feel that it's that way in the gay community too.

These sorts of conversations between Gabrielle and her mom continued sporadically over the course of the next few years, all while Gabrielle continued to identify as bisexual. Over time, she began to understand that her mom was not insisting that she affirm a heterosexual identity; rather, she just wished her daughter would submit to and affirm a gay identity—an identity that she saw in line with her daughter's behavior.

> My mom was finally "well, you're not dating any boys," and I was like "well, I don't know," and she's like "well, are you still bisexual?" and I was like "well, I'm, uh, I'm 60/40," and then it would go to 75/25, and then 80/20, and then, you know, basically I thought I was a lesbian, but I wasn't really sure because I just really wasn't dating guys.

Her rationale for maintaining a bisexual identity was rooted in the fact that she had not *proven*, through concrete action, that dating guys was entirely out of the question. That is, she had not tried dating a boy. By this same logic, most people in society would presently identify as bisexual since they have not attempted to date a member of the same sex. Regardless, her insistence to hold on to both worlds was strong. Although she had not been interested in men at all, it took her years to affirm a lesbian identity. Gabrielle spoke of a conversation that she had with a friend over her MySpace profile which listed her sexuality as "lesbian" despite her insistence that she was bisexual. She recognizes this as the "aha" moment in which she confirmed that she is not attracted to men *at all*—she is a lesbian.

> [Her friend said] "Well, why did [the MySpace profile] say lesbian, like, you told me you were bisexual," and I was like "well, you know, all these guys hit on me . . . I just thought it was fucking annoying that guys were hitting on me, so you know, I put it as lesbian." And she was like "hello, like, ding, ding, ding, ding, doesn't that prove the fact that you are a lesbian, like, hello, Gabby, accept yourself," . . . I was like "wow, I really am a lesbian, ok," and it took a lot—it probably took me like two or three years to really feel comfortable with myself saying "I am Gabby and I am a lesbian."

Adam, a 20 year-old male who presently identifies as gay, faced a similar struggle. He knew that he was interested in men, and completely disinterested in women, but he still insisted on maintaining a bisexual identity—both publicly and privately. Like Gabrielle, his bisexual identity satisfied his personal reliance on holding onto both worlds. It took him quite a while to realize that the bisexual identity did not align with his entirely single-sex (same-sex) interests. His first familial influence came from his mom who maintained a sharply dualistic view on sexuality—either her son was gay or he was straight.

> I initially came out as being bisexual, and I never really came out as being gay . . . I was always . . . [long pause] I came out as bisexual, and I remember sitting down with my mom, and she was like "Adam, you can't be both. It just doesn't work—they're too different. You can't enjoy both. So, at some point you're going to have to pick one." And, I was like {sigh} . . .

The confrontation by Adam's mom really got him thinking about how he identifies.

> That's what really led me to think about "do I really? . . . " I mean, I was 14 at the time, so my world revolved around pornography {laughter} so I was like "do I even watch anything with girls anymore?" I don't hang out with girls . . . I mean, I don't HANG out with girls, but I do hang out with girls. I've never really had a sexual thought about a girl in my life that I can think about.

Even though Adam never had a sexual thought about or even an attraction for a girl, he still identified as bisexual. Only after his mom continued to interrogate him over his sexuality did he finally start to say to himself "you know what, maybe I'm just not [into both boys and girls]." He goes on to say, "I truly *thought* I was bisexual, and it was kind of my mom's pushing that kind of caused me to think deeper on the issue." What Adam did know is that he "liked boys." As he put it "I didn't really know if I liked girls . . . in fact, I didn't think I liked girls, so as far as I was concerned, in the darkness of my own bedroom, I was gay." Later, Adam would come to affirm a publicly gay identity as well.

Discussion and Conclusion

Most people grow up under the impression that to be straight is to be "normal." Influences from outside (family, friends, media, etc.) as well as inside (oneself) encourage those who have same-sex attractions to feel that they must somehow hold on to heterosexuality—at least to a degree. Ten participants in the current study engaged in a queer apologetic—coming out as bisexual despite being interested *only* in members of the same sex. The queer apologetic is essentially a form of identity compromise whereby individuals disclose a bisexual identity that they feel will be palatable to their family, friends, or even themselves. This compromise is based on the rationale that bisexuality simultaneously satisfies 1) their personal attractions for only members of the same sex, and 2) society's expectation that they be attracted to members of the other sex.

The ten individuals who engaged in a queer apologetic came out as bisexual either for the sake of their family/friends or because they were personally not ready to let go of social conventions. Participants whose queer apologetics were based in pleasing family/friends were surprised to find that their family and friends were not supportive of the bisexual identity. Participants were immediately encouraged to affirm a gay identity. The decision to come out initially as bisexual made for a much more difficult route to disclosing their internalized sexuality which eventually aligned with a gay or lesbian identity. Other participants engaged in a queer apologetic based in their own refusal to let go of social conventions. Internalized heteronormativity led these participants to struggle with the realization that they are attracted to members of the same sex and may, in fact, be gay. Rather than coming out as gay, they chose to come out as bisexual, thus allowing them to hold onto "normality." While participants who engaged in a queer apologetic rooted in pleasing family were only engaged in an outward apologetic, participants whose queer apologetic was based in their personal refusal to let go of social conventions were engaged in both an inward and outward apologetic.

While many participants spoke only of their own use of bisexuality as a transitional identity, one male participant engaged in a more detailed analysis why he believes people come out first as bisexual, despite never having been attracted to other sex. Ram, a 21 year-old gay male, explained the practical utility of engaging in a queer apologetic:

> I don't think you go from "in the closet" to "out of the closet." I think there is a, there is a hallway you must walk through, you know. Um, I had it for about 2 days where after I came out to my sister I said "you know, I might be 50/50," which is completely not true, but that's what I was for a couple of days and then the scales slowly tipped and it became 90/10, and then 100/0, 110/-10 for being gay and straight, and I feel like that goes along with the spectrum because it's kind of like I can't leap from straight, even though I was never straight, to gay.

Ram's recollection of the few days he spent under the assumption of being bisexual was both an internal and external apologetic. His family was very traditional, so he had reason to fear the disclosure of a gay identity. But he also needed the quick transitory period in order to process his own reality that he did not have the same sexuality as most other people. His explanation that there was a figurative hallway that he had to walk along as he came out of the metaphorical closet is a clever way to explain the queer apologetic.

A common curiosity among sexuality scholars involves the gendered nature of bisexuality and more specifically homoerotic behavior. Compared to bisexuality among men, bisexuality among women is more socially acceptable (Johnson 2007), and this double standard is rooted heavily in the common (predominantly heterosexual) male fantasy of having sex with two women simultaneously. The paradoxical nature of homoerotic behavior (that it is socially acceptable only if done for the enjoyment of a male heterosexual audience) even influences many women to engage in "performative bisexuality" (Fahs 2011). Research suggests that women do exhibit sexual fluidity more commonly than men (Diamond 2008). Such gender differences may indicate that women are more likely—or at least more inclined—to engage in queer apologetics. The limited sample size in the current study does not allow me to make broad assertions on the basis of gender. However, the current study provides some evidence of sexual fluidity among men, and it suggests that although experiences associated with sexualities may be gendered, the influence of heteronormativity on coming out knows no bounds. Despite the gendered nature of social acceptance regarding bisexuality, men still utilize bisexuality as a transitional identity (i.e., they engage in queer apologetics).

The implications of the queer apologetic go well beyond individuals who engage in such an identity compromise. The people who likely suffer the most are those who earnestly identify as bisexual. Bisexuality is trivialized throughout American culture, and the queer apologetic provides further ammunition for this general lack of acceptance. Society at-large maintains a decidedly dualistic view of sexuality—most people are straight, and those who are not straight are, by default, gay. U.S. culture makes it extremely difficult to live outside of Western dualistic expectations. Bisexuality, as well as intersexuality and transgender, challenges the artificial binaries that society imposes on us all (Crawley et al. 2008; Lucal 2008). The participants in this study—in a roundabout way—demonstrated the principal difficulty associated with maintaining a bisexual identity: people insist on categorizing others dualistically.

Although there appears to be no malicious intent on the part of those who engage in a queer apologetic, this interaction further trivializes bisexuality nonetheless. Rust (1995) provided evidence of bisexual women's frustrations over gay/lesbian women hiding behind bisexuality out of fear, and thus challenging the state of bisexuality as a valid sexual identity. The use of bisexuality as a transitional identity reinforces the essentialist belief in two discrete sexualities, and it perpetuates the common (mis)perception that bisexuality is only a phase and not a true sexual identity. While homosexuality is marginalized in society at large, bisexuality is marginalized even within the LGBTQ community (Bradford 2004). Eden, a participant in the current study who no longer attaches a label to her sexual identity, recalls the hardship of maintaining a bisexual identity, especially around LGBTQ peers:

> I first came out as bisexual, and then I found out, in [the local LGBTQ organization], I was one of two bisexuals in a room of over 50, and then I was starting to hear flying all of these different really negative assumptions about the way I behave as a bisexual—that I don't know what I want or why can't I make a choice.

People who maintain bisexual identities continue to face pressures to "choose a side," and these demands are particularly strong within the LGBTQ community (Ochs 1996; Rust 2000). This reality was discussed by numerous participants. According to Lee, "a lot of homosexuals do not believe in bisexuality, like they take it as an offensive thing . . . like you should just come out already." Lee's statement highlights the primary issue cast upon the bisexual population by the existence of a queer apologetic. Those who use or see bisexuality used as a transitional identity often do not view it as a legitimate sexual identity. Ram, who himself engaged in a queer apologetic, demonstrated the broad lack of acceptance expressed toward bisexuals:

> I think that's really interesting how people, um, don't [come out] right away. I think that the way, um, full blown homosexuals look at bisexual people is interesting, you know, because I used to hate them, you know, that ambivalence, because you can't stereotype, you know, that's probably why, because you can't put them in a box and they're constantly leaking out.

The utilization of bisexuality as a transitional identity causes many people in the LGBQ community, particularly those who engaged in an apologetic themselves, to fail to recognize bisexuality as a concrete identity. This sort of fracturing among the LGBTQ community may, in turn, limit the level of empathy and support received by those with a bisexual identity. Beyond the LGBT community, bisexuality is still relatively invisible (See and Hunt 2011), and the queer apologetic offers one explanation for why this is so.

The queer apologetic also has the potential to help explain why individuals who come out as bisexual (because they earnestly identify as such) may ultimately affirm a gay or lesbian identity that fails to encapsulate their true interests in both men and women. Dualistic thinking trivializes difference on an infinite number of human characteristics. Biracial people are often trivialized as either black or white, intersex people are typically forced to identify as male or female, and bisexuals are encouraged to identify as heterosexual or gay/lesbian. Perhaps the belittling—or de-legitimation—of bisexuality is part of the reason that many queer youth who have affinities for both women and men are opting to affirm pansexual, queer, or fluid identities. These identities, which are still early in their social development, are less broadly understood—hence they may face greater resistance than even bisexuality. But for the time being, these new identities enable people to express difference without taking on the harsh stereotypes that are often associated with bisexuality in the U.S.

People are becoming increasingly open to the existence of non-heterosexual identities, which may lessen the perceived need for an individual to engage in a queer apologetic. Still, people will likely consider engaging in a queer apologetic so long as society maintains a "this or that" mentality. Perhaps with the proliferation of more open interpretations of gender and increased usage of fluid identities, people will opt to come out as pansexual, polysexual, or fluid rather than bisexual. Then again, such open identities are even less understood than bisexuality, which is why five participants in the current study publicly disclosed bisexual identities despite maintaining private identities of pansexual or fluid. The disclosure of any sexual identity outside of heterosexuality would still likely hinder the goal of the queer apologetic: being accepted as "normal." Based on the participants in this study, as people continue along their life trajectories they tend to become increasingly less concerned with what is "normal," "average," or "typical" and therefore work to affirm identities rooted in self-affirmation. Even with the abolition of the heterosexuality-homosexuality dichotomy, individuals who are attracted to members of the same sex may still choose to come out as bisexual (or some other identity that includes both same-sex and other-sex attractions). As long as power and privilege are held by the sexual majority, people may still feel inclined to hold onto heterosexuality—at least to some degree.

---

[1] An earlier version of this chapter appears in a 2013 article entitled "The Queer Apologetic: Explaining the Use of Bisexuality as a Transitional Identity" published in the *Journal of Bisexuality* (Volume 13, Issue 2).

4

Sexual Affinities and Progressive Identities

Sexual identity formation and maintenance has become increasingly central to defining who we are as individuals and groups in society, and cultural perspectives of sexuality are changing accordingly. As is the case with any social construct, the concept of coming out is evolving to keep up with the social and political climate in the United States. Sexual identities have been studied increasingly over the past fifty years, and much is already known about how people affirm and express their sexual identities. My intention with this chapter (and this entire book, for that matter) is not to summarize everything we know about coming out. The purpose and goal here is to engage in a discussion about the many ways in which identity formation and maintenance (and most notably "coming out") is changing in contemporary society. Some would contend that coming out is becoming increasingly irrelevant—particularly as LGBQ identities gain broader acceptance and legitimation. Evidence from the current study suggests that coming out is omnipresent even in relatively affirming environments. We live it a society that is structurally heteronormative; hence, sexual difference is still framed as the exception.

The social phenomenon of coming out is changing in some very important and influential ways. Consider the prior chapter on the queer apologetic. Anecdotally, we often hear of people coming out first as bisexual only to affirm a gay or lesbian identity shortly thereafter. But this is a fairly recent phenomenon. In fact, it was not named, nor did it appear in academic journals until just recently (Guittar 2013b). The queer apologetic is clearly a sign that coming out is changing, and there is other evidence of this as well. From the younger average age at which people come out to the proliferation of newly defined sexual identities, the meanings and utilities of coming out are shifting. Participants in the current study spoke freely about their entire trajectory of coming out—from early affinities to eventual identities. The openness of the interviews resulted in rich data that informs us about every potential facet of coming out as opposed to only the ways in which coming out affects a person's present identity. The themes and trends that make up the "new dynamics" of coming out all emerged from the data without the use of specific interview prompts. Hence these are the themes that appear to be affecting people the most.

Coming Out with Affinity, Not Identity

> It didn't really seem abnormal.
> But it didn't really seem normal either.
> It was just the way it was.
> Oh, okay, so . . . yeah . . . *I just like guys*.
> I kind of want to flaunt it to the world.
> (Teman 2011:875, emphasis added)

Sexual identities are not formed and affirmed overnight. So what do we know about people who are just beginning to recognize having feelings for members of the same sex? Quite simply, we know very little. Literature on coming out is almost exclusively centered on dealing with sexual *identities*. But identities are formed only after people affirm that they are attracted to members of the same sex. That is, they first recognize having a sexual *affinity* for a particular person of the same sex. Upon first recognizing an earnest attraction toward someone of the same sex, many people cite their interest as mere curiosity and they continue to maintain their normative (heterosexual) identity. Based on our culture's heteronormative framework, heterosexuality is familiar and perhaps even comfortable for most people (so much so that it is not even thought about). As a result, individuals who come to realize same-sex attractions oftentimes do not adopt an LGBQ identity immediately. Some people deny these affinities and go about their day. Many others begin to affirm (and perhaps even express to other people) having an *affinity* for members of the same sex. I have come across very little literature that uses the term "affinity" in this way. But I find it to be a very useful tool for encapsulating the way my participants spoke of their early same-sex interests that predated the formation of any LGBQ identities.

Many LGBQ youth are coming out at 15 or 16 years of age—and sometimes even earlier (Grov et al. 2006). It seems logical to consider that not everyone has affirmed a concrete sexual identity at such a young age. This notion is supported by the fact that many participants in the current study came out prior to affirming an LGBQ identity. For example, Rachel came out first as "liking girls" (an affinity) rather than as gay (an identity). Although there exists a variety of reasons for coming out with an affinity, in some cases people are merely coming out before they have realized a specific identity that aligns with their affections. Granted, some queer youth bypass the affirmation of an affinity and opt instead to affirm one of the few monolithic identities that are floating around in our cultural ethos (e.g., gay or bisexual) since they are familiar. But before affirming or, for that matter, even acknowledging an LGBQ identity the first admission most queer youth make is that they are attracted to an individual--someone of the same sex. A teenage girl realizes she is attracted to another girl, or a young woman recognizes earnest romantic interest in another woman. But these early self-admissions are affinities only—they, alone, do not account for shifts in sexual identity. After all, most people do not even think about their sexuality until they have a reason to—and that "reason" is generally that their newfound attractions do not match up with broad cultural expectations regarding traditional sexual arrangements.

I should make another distinction—affinity is not the same as behavior. For example, a young boy may recognize being attracted to another boy at school, but this attraction can persist entirely devoid of any same-sex behavior. Affinities are a matter of, as many participants put it, "liking boys" or "liking girls." According to much of the general U.S. population, behavior—or even affinity—equals identity. So an individual who discloses having same-sex attractions is often assumed to be gay. This unfortunate and erroneous assumption is a result again of dualistic thinking and a firm belief that heterosexual people are "100% straight," and everyone else is, by default, gay. The argument that same-sex affinities or behaviors equal a gay identity also fails the whole methodological dilemma of sufficient cause vs. necessary cause. To explain the distinction between behavior, affinity, and identity I often tell students in my sexuality course the following: someone may attend a Los Angeles Lakers basketball game (behavior) or say that they "like the Lakers" (affinity), but that does not mean s/he is a Lakers fan (identity).

People who have come to the newfound realization that they have an affinity for someone of the same sex likely have not exhibited any behavior or affirmed a new sexual identity. Initially, the self-admission of liking someone of the same sex is nothing more than an affinity for an individual who happens to belong to the same sex category. Thus sexual affinities seem to be the natural precursor to the formation of any concrete sexual identities. To be clear, I am not asserting that the existence of sexual affinities is a new phenomenon. People have likely always recognized being attracted to an individual of the same sex prior to affirming an LGBQ identity. But *coming out via a sexual affinity* (prior to the formation of an LGBQ identity) appears to be an entirely new phenomenon. Contemporary youth are sensing that they can share their affinities with other people and engage in the outward elements of coming out by disclosing to another person: "I like girls," "I like boys," or even "I just like people." Based on data in the current study, mere affinities would not have been enough to encourage someone to come out a few decades ago. Something more concrete would have needed to emerge and dominate an individual's sexuality. Prior cohorts, particularly those who grew up when homosexuality was still defined as a psychological disorder in the DSM, had myriad reasons not to disclose their sexualities until they were absolutely sure they identified as LGBQ (and, depending on their social environments, the same can be said of many LGBQ youth today).

The reality than many youth are coming out with a sexual affinity, not a sexual identity, is a central component of the new trajectory of coming out. The utility of coming out with an affinity is multifold. Some youth are simply choosing to express that they "like boys" or "like girls," and that is all there is to it. Other people are coming out with affinities as a personal or political strategy—a way to "buck the system" that attempts to box us as this identity or that identity. And still others are coming out with affinities as a method of engaging in a queer apologetic. The queer apologetic (Chapter 3) is an individual's attempt at minimizing disapproval of and disappointment over one's sexuality by coming out with an identity (or affinity) that the individual feels will be more easily accepted by family/friends or even oneself. For example, a young girl may come out to her family as "liking girls" under the impression that this affinity would be perceived as much less threatening than if she came out as a lesbian. Affinities are malleable and can give off an air of impermanence, but identities are viewed as absolute and concrete.

Affinities as Personal/Political Strategy

Dualisms are becoming increasingly incapable of encapsulating identities, particularly in terms of sexuality. Plenty of people interpret their sexuality as what Michael Messner (2007) calls "100% straight." That is, they leave no wiggle room—they are absolutely, unequivocally straight. They are attracted to members of the other sex—end of discussion. In the same vein, many gay and lesbian women and men stake their claim of being 100% gay. The take-away from these two trends is that most Americans are decidedly "100%" in their claims toward their sexual identities—they inhabit one polar extreme or the other. The maintenance of these polarizing views contributes to identity politics which do not allow for "intermediate" identities, multiple-sex attractions, or progressive/fluid identities. In fact, many Americans—both gay and straight—do not feel that any other identities (e.g., bisexuality, pansexuality, etc.) exist. To some degree, the Western world is beginning to move beyond the dualistic categorizations of sexuality. At the very least, we have experienced the popularization of a third identity, bisexuality. By no means is bisexuality fully embraced or even understood by society at large (See and Hunt 2011). Still, bisexuality has been established as a viable identity that can exist outside of the "100%" dualisms discussed above. Emergent identities such as fluid, pansexual, queer and polysexual have given individuals a greater sense of affirming an identity that does not trivialize their own unique sexualities.

In the struggle to carve out unique identities which fill the void between gay and straight, some people are choosing to opt out of identity games altogether, and speak instead of their sexuality free of definitions. Rather than affirming a concrete *sexual identity* (i.e., "I am gay") some individuals are choosing to express a *sexual affinity* for members of the same sex (i.e., "I like girls"). This expression of choosing to be unlabeled, and thereby free of commitment to a specific identity, is aimed at remaining "unboxed." Such a stance was demonstrated by a handful of participants in Yon-Leau and Munoz-Laboy's (2011) study of sexuality politics among Latino youth. As one such participant, Francisco, stated:

> I don't like defining myself, it's too much, its I just don't like labels. *I do like guys*, though I don't think it should be just labeled but in society's views I'm a homosexual . . . I mean love shouldn't have boundaries (quoted in Yon-Leau and Munoz-Laboy 2011:117, emphasis added).

So the decision to affirm or express an affinity (in Francisco's case, "liking guys") is aimed explicitly at operating outside of the constraints of a label. But, more often than not, it seems that people who express only an affinity for members of the same sex (as opposed to expressing a sexual identity) face a great deal of opposition from other people to choose a box. Again, the popular (false) assumption is that "same-sex affinities = a gay identity."

Kelly, a 22 year-old participant in the current study speaks volumes about the pressure she confronts to attach a label to her sexuality.

> Sometimes I feel pressured to, you know, identify, and people will ask me "well, what are you?" Because I've dated guys in the past but I currently have a girlfriend so, um, a lot of times people will be like "oh, you're a lesbian for right now," and I'm just like "you know, no, that's not true, and I don't appreciate that," but I do chuckle at it sometimes. But, um, yeah, I kind of feel pressured to label myself, which kind of mixes me up mentally, and I'm like do I need to identify? Does it matter? But most of the time I'm just like "uh, it's whatever. I'm just me."

Prior to Kelly's discussion of other people insisting that she attach herself to an LGBQ identity, I had asked her how she identified her sexuality. As she conveyed:

> I actually still don't even know how I identify. Um, so that's still kind of up in the air, because I, like you said I don't like to identify myself, so, um, I guess people have identified me for myself . . . I like, I like people. That's usually what I just say "I like people," and they laugh and that's usually the end of it. I mean, for people who know me at least, and other people who don't really know me and don't . . . like, a lot of people know my politics even. Um, I guess I'm very up-front about it, so a lot of people understand who I am and what I stand for, but if they don't they'll be more inclined to ask questions and I'll go into the whole like "you don't need to put me in a box," you know.

At the onset of my interviews I asked participants the following question: "What is your self-identified sexual orientation?" Based on the responses to this question provided by five queer or pansexual participants (including Kelly) it is clear that many people prefer to express their sexuality via a sexual affinity. Among these five participants, the preference for expressing a sexual affinity rather than a sexual identity is based in the sense that most people simply do not understand their "progressive, open" sexualities. Kelly, as well as the other four individuals, admitted that she sometimes does express a sexual identity simply to appease other people.

Eden, a 22 year-old woman who chooses not to identify her sexuality at all, similarly spoke of her desire to express affinities and stray from utilizing labels.

> I don't identify at all. I choose not to identify because I do not like fitting into a box. I don't like adhering to a label that I know has lots of

stereotypes and negative connotations around it, so I refuse to identify. There is . . . it's difficult because when you label your sexuality it helps people understand where you're coming from a little bit better. But, I feel like if I can explain why I don't use a label it does the same thing . . . I like who I like for who they are.

Under these circumstances, the utilization of *affinities* in order to convey one's sexuality is a personal, political decision aimed at remaining true to oneself and not caving in to the wants of society-at-large. But, as Eden points out, labels are beneficial since they often serve an important role in conveying one's sexuality to another person. Sexual identities are prescribed labels that provide a shared sense of to whom someone is attracted and they convey a sense of where someone stands politically in many cases. But sexual identities are also seen as concrete—and can therefore come off as much more threatening to family or friends whom individuals believe to be less accepting of LGBQ identities. Such is why many youth may choose to come out to other people (even oneself) with an affinity rather than an identity as a form of identity compromise (i.e., a queer apologetic).

Affinity and the Apologetic

As we saw in Chapter 3, individuals often come out with public sexualities that differ from their internalized sexualities. Recall Adam, who, despite only ever being interested in men, came out initially as bisexual. His decision to do so was rooted in the belief that his parents would be more accepting of a bisexual identity than a gay identity. He hypothesized that bisexuality would enable his parents to hold out hope that he might engage in future relationships with women. Rather than disclosing a public sexual *identity* that aligns with their private sexuality, people sometimes opt to come out first with an *affinity* for the same sex[1]. Just as with the disclosure of a bisexual identity, the technique of coming out with affinity allows the individual to keep the door open on the possibility of future relationships with members of the other sex. When I speak of "coming out with affinity" rather than an identity, I am referring to participants saying to themselves and others that they "like" a particular category of people (i.e., "girls/women" or "boys/men"). This sort of language was peppered throughout the interviews, most notably among the participants who engaged in a queer apologetic (for a greater discussion of the queer apologetic, see Chapter 3).

One of the clearest examples of how affinities are often used when engaging in a queer apologetic was demonstrated by Rachel, a young woman who came out first with an affinity ("liking girls"), later as bisexual, and then eventually as gay. When I asked her about her experiences with coming out Rachel quickly responded, "at first I just said 'I like girls'." In explaining her rationale, Rachel explained that she "would tell people, you know, that I like girls, but I never said 'hey I'm gay,' or 'I'm a lesbian,' so I kind of 'I like girls,' that's how I kind of brought it up to people." In her purview, affinities were less threatening to other people and she thought that coming out simply as "liking girls" would allow her to avoid being stereotyped by her peers. Based on the reactions of other people, Rachel grew quickly aware of the fact that other people wished to see her express a more concrete identity (namely a gay identity). In one conversation with her mother she expressed that she was attracted to women and after sensing that her mother was not content with this admission, Rachel quickly altered her message and stated "'I'm bi-' . . . just to make it easier." But her mother kept drilling her with questions like "well, what do you think you are?" Rachel's intention for coming out with an affinity was to express her attraction to women while still allowing other people to maintain a belief that she could engage in relationships with men in the future. But she eventually felt the pressure to adopt a more concrete sexual identity that appeased other people, and she did so accordingly.

Rachel was not alone in her usage of affinities in order to attempt to please other people. Two other young women, Kyle and Ari, initially came out to friends and family as "liking girls." Kyle's first admission to another person that she was not explicitly heterosexual took place during a conversation with her sister. Rather plainly, she recalls, "I was like 'I kind of like girls.'" She proceeded to come out to other people as "liking girls" even as she began to understand that she was interested only in women—a realization which led her to eventually affirm a lesbian identity. Ari relied similarly on coming out with an affinity, but her mode of communication was even less direct. Typically, she did not initiate any conversations about her sexuality. Instead, her admission that she liked women came only after someone else questioned her sexuality. "It's not so much me saying 'I'm bisexual,' as much as it is [someone else asking] 'do you like girls?' and I respond 'yes.'" This still classifies as coming out with affinity because during none of these early encounters did Ari confirm, or rather affirm, a sexual identity. Ari also demonstrated a unique variation of coming out with affinity. Rather than coming out to her mother as "liking girls" she came out to her as "not liking guys."

> I just exploded into tears and I was like "you know, before I tell you this, I just want you to remember that I'm your daughter and I love you," and she's like "yes, I know, and I love you too . . . what's wrong?" And I told her "ok, well *I don't really like guys* (emphasis added).

Ari's admission that she is not attracted to men belongs with the common thread of "liking girls/women", but it conveys a greater amount of information. Whereas "liking girls" would have still left the door open for dating members of the other sex, Ari's admission that she does not like guys whatsoever actually affirms a gay identity (assuming she believes in the existence of only two sex categories) since it implies that she only likes women. Still, this language is less concrete than saying "I'm gay," which is a big part of why she chose to speak in such a way.

While Rachel, Kyle, and Ari come out initially with an affinity in an attempt to please other people, some participants came out with an affinity because they themselves were not ready to affirm an LGBQ identity. The best example of this interaction was demonstrated by Veronica, who grew up in a very affirming environment. Despite having a family that was familiar and comfortable with issues involving the LGBTQ community, Veronica still grappled with her own internal desire to "hold onto normality." As she put it, "my first thought wasn't 'oh, I'm totally gay,' it was just *admitting that I liked girls*." Since she was not affirming or expressing a specific sexual identity, Veronica allowed herself to refrain from closing the door on other-sex relations. In the months following, Veronica began to slowly move past her internalized heteronormativity as she soon came out as bisexual, and eventually as a lesbian. In reflecting on her experiences Veronica saw her decision to come out with an affinity as a natural first step which slowly got her more and more comfortable with being attracted only to women.

Another participant, Pao, recalled a similar motivation to come out with an affinity. Pao spoke about a conversation she had with her best friend regarding why she appeared so unhappy all the time:

> [My friend] sat me down and she was like "Pao, I want you to tell me what's wrong because you're just, like, bad, you look really bad." I ended up telling her, I said "I'm in love with [another friend] and I like girls."

You may remember from Chapter 3 that Pao grew up in a very homophobic environment. However, she recalls being unaffected by the disapproval of other people regarding her sexuality. It was her own internal refusal to affirm an LGBQ identity that led her to come out with an affinity for quite some time before coming out as bisexual, and eventually gay.

Among all of the men in this study, Lee was the only one who recalled coming out with an affinity. For quite some time Lee was not willing to consider the affirmation of a gay identity. Thus, he self-affirmed and came out to others with an affinity.

> The first time I really came out to someone that I feel that I could talk about my sexuality was with my best friend. I was just like "I need to tell you something," and she's like "oh, what is it." And I was just like "*I like guys.*"

Lee's internalized heteronormativity prevented him from affirming a gay identity for quite some time. You may be thinking to yourself "don't you mean to say that Lee was suffering from internalized homophobia?" The simple answer is no. Lee was very affirming of and close friends with a large group of LGBQ peers—hence he harbored no sense of homophobia. However, he did internalize the normative formation of "man + woman = normal" for himself. Hence, he suffered the repercussions of internalizing these heteronormative beliefs. Again, all of the examples in this section are from participants who previously engaged in a queer apologetic in an attempt to minimize disappointment over or disapproval of their sexuality. The trend of coming out first as "liking girls/boys" is sometimes rooted in this same interaction—limiting the potential backlash of eventually disclosing an LGBQ identity.

Coming out with affinity (e.g., liking girls) is less concrete and therefore less threatening to much of society than coming out with an LGBQ identity. Coming out with an affinity allows family, friends, even oneself to maintain the possibility that other-sex partner may still be a possibility in the future. So all of those expectations that have been building up since childhood (both personal and familial) may still be kept intact. Another form of coming out with affinity that was demonstrated across multiple interviews related to coming out as bi-curious or as questioning. Although we commonly hear references to "bi-curious" and "questioning" as sexual identities, the relative impermanence of these labels mirrors affinities in many ways. Gabrielle, who came out initially as bi-curious (and sometimes as "liking girls") recalls:

I told [my mom] I was bi-curious and she was like "ok, that's cool," and I was like "oh, ok," and then two weeks later I was like "I'm bisexual," and then she flipped out because it was more legitimate.

Parental reactions are remarkably different between coming out as bi-curious (exploration) versus bisexual (identity). As was the case with Gabrielle's mom, bi-curious is often shrugged off as just what the label implies: curiosity. Bi-curious and questioning lack the degree of permanence that is implied by other sexual identities. The decidedly negative reaction of Gabrielle's mother to her later expressing a bisexual identity is also a great example of the motivation for participants to come out first as liking girls/boys rather than come out with a concrete identity. It minimizes confrontation and enables individuals to put less strain on their relationships with the people they count on most.

Affinities satisfy the needs of the person coming out since they allow the individual to express their same-sex interests without coming off as nearly as threatening to family and friends. The same can be said of those who came out as being bi-curious or questioning—identities which suggest mere curiosity and a sense of impermanence. As soon as participants moved beyond affinity or curiosity and offered up a more concrete identity it sent a clear message to others that this is more than just a phase. And as seen in the queer apologetic, family members were—to the surprise of many participants—not willing to affirm the individual's affinity or intermediate (bisexual) identity. Participants recall sensing that it was a good idea, a compromise, but family and friends eventually demanded that the individual affirm a gay identity since it fits our typical dualistic logic.

The pattern of coming out with affinities—regardless of the motivations for doing so—is also evidence of how the increasingly younger age at which people come out has an effect on coming out itself. Younger individuals are less likely to have affirmed a concrete sexual identity, which may help explain why this new form of coming out (with affinity) has emerged very prominently in the narratives of the participants in this study. Another element of coming out which is quickly emerging is the reality that people today are commonly engaged in multiple "coming outs."

Multiple "Coming Outs"

> I think, as a gay person, there's always multiple coming outs. I mean, every person I meet on the fucking street, you know, if they realize I'm gay [they're like] "You're gay?"—"Yeah, I'm gay,"—once again, that's another coming out.

~Gabrielle

There is a lot of rhetoric in our culture about sexuality being a fairly straight-forward, clear-cut part of our identities. And this may have once been the case (or at least appeared to be the case). As our understanding of sexuality has improved, we have come to recognize just how fluid human sexuality may be. We have also come to understand that coming out is much more complex and variable from person-to-person than was previously thought. When we commonly hear of people coming out multiple times, we often think of that which Gabrielle is speaking about in the quote above. LGBQ persons often find themselves coming out to many different people in many different social situations. Gabrielle was speaking primarily about her recognition that she has to engage in coming out at sporadic times—in her daily interactions with just anyone, a stranger on the street, a co-worker, a classmate. Suzanne Johnson, a college professor who interacts with new people on campus all the time, spoke of this same realization in her article about what she calls her "revolving closet door":

> I constantly rotate through varying degrees of revelation and exposure. It's like having a continuously moving revolving door on a closet. I've come to decide that, for me, a revolving door is the best type of door to have on a closet. It's always moving, it's never closed, and you can always see inside (Johnson 2008: 66-67).

It is evident that coming out does not take place at just a single point in time (although popular media might inform us otherwise). Self-affirmation and the outward disclosure of one's sexuality can result in coming out multiple times—perhaps even to the same people. This is particularly true when you consider the reality shared by many participants in this study: that coming out is a *career* (more on this in Chapter 6).

Most intriguing about the notion of "multiple coming outs" is the fact that people are increasingly coming out multiple times to the *same people*, and even themselves. Historically, a great deal of literature on coming out assumed that sexual identities are static, fixed entities (e.g., person A is gay, so person A comes out to person B—and now person B "knows"). But, sexual identities are not so fixed. In fact, they are rather fluid, and this fluidity translates to LGBQ persons often coming out multiple times to some of the same people. Consider Gabrielle's admission:

> I came out as bi-curious, and then I came out as bisexual . . . It took a lot . . . It probably took me like two or three years to really feel comfortable with myself saying "I am Gabby and I am a lesbian," and now I am, you know, so I think it was definitely a process.

Gabrielle is demonstrating a level of fluidity that was quite common among the participants in this study. Most often, people cited the desire to "hold onto normality," or the desire to keep the dreams and expectations of their family and friends alive. Now, the desire to please others or blend into the crowd is not necessarily a new thing—these motivations for human interaction are likely as old as human civilization itself. What makes the maintenance of modern sexualities different from decades past is that people today are more likely to come out shortly after affirming a new sexual identity (or affinity). Take for example, Gabrielle, who affirmed and came out publicly after each of four shifts in her sexuality: 1) "liking girls," 2) bi-curious, 3) bisexual, and then 4) as a lesbian. Historically people were likely to refrain from coming out until they had a more fixed sense of their identity—perhaps having affirmed that identity for a longer period of time before sharing their sexuality with others. As seen in our discussion of sexual affinities, this is no longer the case. Nine different participants came out initially to their family, their friends, and in some cases even themselves with an affinity. Five of these individuals have since affirmed gay or lesbian identities while the other four have maintained relatively open identities of queer or pansexual, or they do not attach themselves to any specific identity. Of the nine participants who came out first with an affinity, each one of them later came out to the same people with their newly affirmed sexual identities. Hence they came out 2, 3, even 4 times to the same people.

The process of moving through multiple identities and coming out after affirming each identity is not only about the outward elements of coming out—that is, coming out to others. As Gabrielle demonstrated above, she came out multiple times to herself as well. In fact, more than half of the participants in this study volunteered to me that they came out multiple times to themselves as well as to other people. One sexual identity (or an affinity) may have remained for a few months, only to be replaced by a new identity, and so on. For fifteen participants, bisexuality was the first sexual identity affirmed and expressed. Ten of the participants who came out first as bisexual later affirmed a gay or lesbian identity. These are the same ten people who were the center of our discussion of the queer apologetic—they came out multiple times to the same people, and some of them even self-affirmed multiple identities across time (recall that some of the people who engaged in a queer apologetic did so only for the sake of other people—these individuals never shifted their private identities, only their public identities).

Those participants who cited coming out after each identity they self-affirmed consisted exclusively of people who were born after 1988. For example, young women like Kyle were the ones who came out initially as "liking girls," then as bisexual, and finally as a lesbian—thus resulting in multiple "outings" to many of the same people. Ari and Veronica demonstrated a similar trajectory of coming out multiple times after affirming new identities. Lisa Diamond's (2004) research on sexual fluidity reinforces that this is rather common for young women. But coming out multiple times with different identities is not limited to women. In the current study, it was also demonstrated by four men: Adam, Lee, Ram and to a lesser degree, Brian. For instance, Ram came out as bi-curious, then bisexual, and eventually gay. His multiple coming outs were simply about him trying to ease people into the idea that he was attracted to men. Ram spoke about this at great length:

> I would say I never had a perfect coming out story with any one person, it's always been kind of like tapping on the brakes. You know, you've got to sort of feel your way through it. I had to come out to my parents several times because the first time it was just "no, no it's a phase, blah, blah, blah," you know, but it's definitely jerky . . .

Still, the young men in the sample did exhibit some sexual fluidity, even though there were far more women who spoke of shifting identities over time. Research has already hinted at sexual fluidity among men, but not necessarily in this same sense. With the exception of Brian, the sexual fluidity demonstrated by the men in this study all relate to their shifting identities (or affinities)—thus giving the impression that sexuality is malleable and apt to change over time. Brian earnestly expressed sexual fluidity, and he even spoke about how he commonly came out as gay simply because he did not believe other people would understand that men can be queer or fluid. As he explained:

> I definitely specifically came out to [my family] as gay, even though I
> identify as queer and, like, I've slept with women before and, like
> bisexual, more like fluid, but I didn't want them to think that I was just
> going through a phase because I know they're not too open-minded
> with, like, things like that.

But the narratives of the other three men (Adam, Lee, and Ram)
provided only the *appearance* of sexual fluidity—that is, their "fluidity"
may really be nothing more than a showcase of how coming out
trajectories are constantly influenced by heteronormativity. Throughout
their interviews these three men expressed never being attracted to
anyone other than men, even though their publicly expressed sexual
identities shifted over time from identities that allowed for other-sex
attractions to identities rooted solely in same-sex attractions (i.e., gay
identities). The fluidity seen among these men echoes the outward
elements of the queer apologetic—utilizing various identities in order to
gradually "let go of normality." Of course, let us not assume that these
men's identities are final, authentic identities that will cease to change
further in the future.

Only the younger participants in this study exhibited "multiple
coming outs" that were rooted in coming out with new identities over
time. Participants born prior to 1988 almost exclusively reported having
come out only after they affirmed their present identity. Any time
participants in this older cohort spoke of "multiple coming outs" they
were speaking of coming out to many different people, but not multiple
times to the same people. Basically, older cohorts came out only after
their identities were perceived as being absolutely solidified—whereas
younger cohorts were more likely to come out as soon as they affirmed
an affinity or identity that included same-sex attractions, after which
they came out again following any subsequent changes in identity.

Eden, like Ari, Veronica, and Gabrielle, came out multiple times
with different identities as well. But the motives behind the changes in
her sexuality were mostly based in clarifying others' misconceptions of
her sexuality and trying to keep others from trivializing her experiences.

> I first came out as bisexual, and then I found out, in [a college LGBTQ
> group], I was one of two bisexuals in a room of over 50, and then I
> was starting to hear flying all of these different really negative
> assumptions about the way I behave as a bisexual—that I don't know
> what I want or why can't I make a choice, or anything like that. So,
> then I decided that I'd be polysexual, meaning I like who I like
> whether they're transgender or male or female as their gender, but then
> even that people kind of think that you are a floozy . . . that you just

kind of will sleep around with anybody at any time, so then I got sick
of the whole show and now I don't identify myself.

Eden came out first as bisexual, then as polysexual, and currently she
attaches no identity to her sexuality. Her philosophy toward her own
sexuality never really changed. Essentially, she likes who she likes—end
of story. What did change was her public presentation of that identity,
which many people still have a hard time accepting or even
understanding (this was cited as a common challenge associated with
maintaining a newly-formed, progressive identity in general). Despite
the fact that new identities (e.g., pansexual) are less understood across
society, they are gaining popularity in that they more accurately reflect
how individuals truly identify. Of particular interest here is the way in
which the affirmation of progressive identities—pansexual, fluid,
polysexual, and, to a lesser degree, queer—affects coming out.

The Proliferation of Progressive Identities

The average American is unaccustomed to hearing about sexual
identities such as pansexual, polysexual, and fluid. For the most part,
people tend to understand two identities—heterosexual and gay (or
lesbian). Even bisexuality, a sexuality that has been a part of our cultural
dialog for quite some time, is not widely understood (much less
embraced). Part of the difficulty associated with disclosing a bisexual
identity is that few people understand bisexuality. The common
sentiment is that bisexuals are confused or still figuring things out, or
they just need to pick a side (such was expressed by many gay/lesbian
participants in the current study). Bisexuality remains marginalized
partly because the meaning of bisexuality varies substantially from
person to person. For one individual, it means having concurrent
attractions for both men and women, while for another it simply means
having episodic interest in relationships with one sex or the other
(McLean 2007). Perhaps most importantly, bisexuality is marginalized
because we tend to assume someone's sexuality based on what we see in
a given moment. A woman who is seen intimately with a man is
assumed to be heterosexual, and a woman whose partner is also a
woman is assumed to be gay. Bisexuality cannot be identified in such a
way.

Still, the benefit of bisexual identities, as well as lesbian and gay
identities, is that people understand them better than other sexual
identities simply because they conform to our common dualistic
divisions of sex (female/male) and gender (woman/man). A gay man is

attracted to other gay men. A bisexual woman is attracted, in some form, to both men and women. The same cannot be said about the identities of pansexual, polysexual, fluid, and, to a lesser degree, queer. For individuals who affirm one of these identities, sex or gender may not be used as a factor in determining to whom they are attracted, or they may not view sex and gender as having the simple, dichotomous division used by the majority of society. Further contributing to the trivialization of these newly emergent identities is the fact that we typically judge others based upon what we see at any given moment. Regardless of whether people identify as pansexual, polysexual, queer, or bisexual, individuals who are engaged in same-sex relationships are perceived by much of society to be gay or lesbian.

Prior to speaking more about the proliferation of these newly emergent identities, it is helpful to provide a basic understanding of how participants utilized these labels. For example, what is a queer identity, and how is it explained to other people upon coming out? What does pansexual or polysexual mean to someone who identifies as such? Rather than relying on outside sources, let us consider the ways in which the participants in this study utilize and define these sexualities.

"Queer" is an identity that may or may not be hard to explain to other people, but it is quickly becoming more prevalent (consider that many LGBT groups have, over the past few years, begun to assert that they are now LGBTQ groups). In the most basic sense, the word "queer" is used to communicate that an individual's sexuality is anything other than explicitly heterosexual or an individual's gender may not conform to our traditional gender expectations (i.e., "queer = different"). Queer is sometimes used in place of gay, and other times it is used by someone who would not identify with any label otherwise. Oftentimes participants who privately identify with a newly emerging identity (such as queer) indicated coming out to other people as gay because society still maintains a strong gay/straight binary. This interaction was demonstrated by Brian, a man who is attracted only to men, but who identifies as queer. "I identify as queer, but it depends who I'm talking with and sometimes I just identify as gay just because it's a lot easier." Brian's admission goes back to a point made earlier: individuals often disclose public identities that they perceive to be more palatable to others than the internal identities they affirm. Unlike people who express bisexual identities via a queer apologetic, Brian's disclosure of a gay identity is typically more well-received. Another participant, H.G., expanded on the decision process that goes into choosing whether to express a queer or gay identity. When asked how he identifies, he responded:

> Normally, I would say gay because that's what people are going to offer. Um, I probably identify as queer more than anything, but that's not very popular, and that's very offensive to a lot of people . . . you have your orientation checklist, it's usually going to be GLBT kind of stuff, so usually gay. I think most of the students I work with, I know you said to talk about me, but most of them are very comfortable with the word queer, but if you look at people in my generation they're not at all. In fact, my boss hates the word, but to her it's a very derogatory word. And to me it's a word where I really don't have to explain a lot. It's, to me, queer is "different", so that's me.

H.G. noted a very important characteristic of the queer identity. The word "queer" itself has a very polarizing history. In contemporary society, queer is an empowering identity for many LGBTQ persons, but it is also a pejorative used by homophobic boys/men who wish to demean others whom they see as less than the pinnacle of masculinity (see C.J. Pascoe's body of research on this unfortunate trend). With this in mind I often tell my students that queer is both an empowering adjective and a demeaning noun.

Brian and H.G. may both identify as queer, but their use of this identity differs sharply from other participants such as Carly, a 22 year-old graduate student. In a perfect world, Carly would likely not attach any label to her sexuality. Her personal trajectory hints at a belief in sexual fluidity and gender fluidity. Queer is an identity which encompasses both types of fluidity very well. Recall that, in its most basic form, queer means different. After explaining to me that she identifies as queer, she went on to explain why the queer identity best encapsulates her sexuality:

> I feel that queer is kind of an umbrella term more. Um, because I don't like to identify as a lesbian because I've dated boys and I don't think that I am attracted to just women. I feel like, I'm one of those people who thinks that gender and sexuality are very fluid and there's not just two genders and there's not just two sexualities. I don't to say, and that's why I don't say bisexual either, because then it's like, I'm not just like, I don't like "boys and girls," *shrugging*. I don't really understand or completely, I mean maybe someday I'll identify as something else besides queer because I don't really know what I'm going to be or what I'm going to feel later.

Carly's affirmation of a queer identity allows her to express an identity that places her firmly within the LGBTQ community, while also allowing her the flexibility to not feel so "boxed." Carly's identification as queer is also remarkably similar to the ways in which other participants utilized pansexual and polysexual identities.

Pansexuality and polysexuality have a lot in common. In fact, their interpretations by participants in this study were almost identical. During every interview in which pansexuality or polysexuality was discussed I heard phrases such as "I like who I like," or "I just like people." This sentiment is also common among people who choose not to identify at all (such as Ruby). Kelly is another participant who honestly prefers not to attach an identity to her sexuality, but she often explains to others that she is pansexual in order to appease those who insist that she explain her sexuality via a specific sexual identity. According to Kelly, pansexuality does not have anything to do with gender. In expressing that she is pansexual, she is communicating to other people that gender is not part of the equation in determining to whom she is attracted. Rather, her attractions go across (i.e., "pan-") all gender categories. This perspective is very difficult for her to explain to other people since most Americans view gender as an early prerequisite in determining to whom they are attracted. Further, most Americans refuse to consider the presence of more than two genders or sexes. Although Kelly often comes out with an affinity, whenever she does convey a sexual identity, she comes out as pansexual. As she conveyed:

> I actually still don't even know how I identify. Um, so that's still kind of up in the air . . . I don't like to identify myself, so, um, I guess people have identified me for myself, so I guess other people have identified me as being bisexual, but I think I'm more pansexual just because I love people, it doesn't matter. [Pansexuality] doesn't have anything to do with, yeah, gender at all or how they identify. It's based more off of personality and how I get along with them.

It is this progressive view of gender that most often leads others to try and simplify Kelly's sexuality as bisexual. They see her with a man or they see her with a woman—in the eyes of the average person, liking both men and women amounts to bisexuality. Of course, if people judge her sexuality based upon only her current relationship with another woman, then she is assumed to be gay. This is the same reason that Eden, who previously came out as bisexual and then polysexual, no longer expresses a sexual identity when coming out to others.

Harsh stereotypes and myths about Kelly's dating trajectory (which involved partners of multiple genders) led her to abandon all labels. Kelly cited a similar expectation from other people that she accept the identities that others cast upon her:

Sometimes I feel pressured to, you know, identify, and people will ask me "well, what are you?" because I've dated guys in the past but I currently have a girlfriend so, um, a lot of times people will be like "oh, you're a lesbian for right now," and I'm just like "you know, no, that's not true, and I don't appreciate that," but I do chuckle at it sometimes. But, um, yeah, I kind of feel pressured to label myself, which kind of mixes me up mentally, and I'm like "do I need to identify? Does it matter?" but most of the time I'm just like "uh, it's whatever. I'm just me."

Considering how often Kelly is encouraged to identify as bisexual or some other identity, it is not surprising that students in my sexuality courses often ask me how you can tell if people identify as bisexual versus pansexual. My gut instinct is to tell students "why does it matter to you? It's their lives, not yours." But in all honestly, I tell them that you simply cannot tell—at least not as a passive observer on the outside looking in. The differences between bisexuality and pansexuality are not observable characteristics. They are held by the individual who identifies as such, and that's that. But when you get into a discussion of sexual identities that include progressive views of gender (such as with pansexuality) you find this sort of question to be quite common. In the end, many people who identify as pansexual, polysexual, or fluid opt to identify as Kelly did above: "I'm just me." Ruby, Eden, and Carly exhibited this same sort of response, as they often express affinities rather than identities as a way of conveying that they like who they like and that is all there is to it. This ideology becomes the basis of a mantra that a few of my participants (namely those with newly emerging identities) live by: *live life openly and honestly.*

Being Open & Honest

In the eyes of Eden, Ruby, Kyle, Kelly, and Pao, coming out is very much about being open and honest. These two words, "open" and "honest," were central to many discussions of coming out, particularly among participants who held more progressive views of gender and sexuality. This sense of openness and honesty relates to external as well as internal elements of coming out. The mantra is rooted in a belief that there is value in sticking to your guns and identifying—both publicly and privately—the way *you* truly identify. Sexual identities need not fit the handful of ascribed labels proffered by society-at-large. Sexuality is about being true to you, and not hiding or contorting anything about yourself. Usage of "open" and "honest" was most common among participants who viewed coming out as being primarily a matter of self-affirmation (these individuals spoke primarily about being honest to themselves). To a lesser degree, openness was also spoken about among participants who felt conversely that coming out was a matter of full disclosure to others (these individuals spoke mostly of being open and honest to everyone they met).

The use of language like "living openly and honestly" or "living my life honestly" was not limited to a handful of participants—in all, 16 participants made some reference to this ideology. In many cases, the words "open" and "honest" were simply woven into the fabric of participants' language. For example, Kyle, a 21 year-old who identifies as a lesbian, spoke about how coming out meant "being open with oneself and others about who you truly are." Another participant, Ruby, a 24 year-old woman who chooses not to identify her sexuality, sums up coming out in similar terms: "I guess it's just honesty. It's just being honest about who you are. You can come out as anything, you know, but it's just being honest about how you are in terms of feelings toward other people."

The common thread among participants who used the words "open" or "honest" in great volume was that these individuals were less concerned with the acceptance of other people. Their journey, and therefore the meaning they attribute to coming out, was more about coming to grips with their own unique sexuality rather than explaining it to other people in terms that fit outsiders' perspectives of gender and sexuality. Coming out to oneself was central to the meaning they ascribed to coming out, and this was particularly true among individuals who identified their sexual orientations as queer, fluid, pansexual, or not identified. Quite simply, since much of society does not understand sexualities like pansexual or fluid, coming out becomes rooted almost entirely in honestly self-affirming their relatively progressive identities.

Research suggests that coming out to other people is more of a necessity for people who are interested only in members of the same sex (i.e., gay or lesbian) than it is for bisexuals (McLean 2007). In the case of bisexuality or various open identities (e.g., pansexual, fluid), individuals are not as easily identifiable on the basis of with whom they engage in relationships. Considering our society's insistence on binary logic (gay/straight, male/female) those who have attractions for both men and women, multiple genders, or those who do not use gender as a determinate for choosing a mate are often misunderstood. The socially constructed, dualistic framework makes coming out more problematic for individuals who are bisexual, queer, fluid or pansexual. Difficulty in explaining and justifying a sexual identity that is rooted in multiple attractions leads many people to make a choice: a) come out publicly with an identity that others understand even if it does not match one's true internal sexuality, or b) focus on self-acceptance and place less emphasis on coming out to others via a specific identity. More often than not, those who speak of living "openly and honestly" choose the latter.

Eden is a perfect example of de-emphasizing the external side of coming out and choosing to focus almost exclusively on being honest with oneself. Eden truly advocates living her life "openly and honestly." In fact, she used such language more than any other participant. Eden prefers to no longer identify. She had previously been misunderstood and stereotyped each time she expressed a particular sexual identity—in her case bisexual and later polysexual. Eden's open view of sexuality now places much more of the onus of coming out on self-acceptance and self-affirmation—essentially coming out to oneself. As Eden further articulated:

> I know I say this a lot, but this is kind of my life mantra—to live openly and honestly—and that's what coming out means to me . . . If you say "I live my life openly and honestly" then you're not going to shun other people for their belief systems. [Coming out means to] live your life openly and honestly when appropriate in a happy, healthy environment not impeding on other people's standpoints . . . the way I abbreviate it is "live your life openly and honestly."

Eden advocates being open and affirming of other people's sexualities as much as she speaks of being honest to herself. In essence these two modes of thinking go hand-in-hand. Perhaps as more and more people affirm identities such as pansexual, polysexual, or no identity at all, we will see an increase in the overall acceptance of sexuality as the personal, private element of one's life that it should be. Then again, depending on the social and political climate of sexualities in the U.S. these identities may simply become the most marginalized contingent of a larger marginalized population. Only time will tell.

Discussion and Conclusion

Much is changing in terms of how people affirm their sexual identities, and even more so how they express their sexual identities to other people. In accordance with the increasingly younger age at which people are coming out, individuals are frequently coming out by affirming and (if desired) disclosing that they have an affinity for members of the same sex. This technique of coming out with affinity, not identity, allows the individual to keep the door open on the possibility of future other-sex relationships. It is also typically perceived, among participants in this study, to be more palatable to other people. People with newfound affections for members of the same sex utilized language such as "liking girls/women" or "liking boys/men" or just "liking people" in order to initially express or communicate their sexualities to friends, family, and in some cases even themselves. For example, Lee came out first to his best friend as liking guys. "I was just like 'I need to tell you something,' and she's like 'oh, what is it.' And I was just like '*I like guys*.'"

Nine participants in this study spoke of coming out first with an affinity, and this was most common among participants who engaged in a queer apologetic. Coming out with affinity rather than identity was seen by many participants as the safest way to come out, especially when they have yet to form a concrete sexual identity. This is a theme that emerged naturally from conversation about coming out. It appears to clearly be a central component of many people's trajectories regarding coming out. Although it came up in exactly nine of my interviews, based on the similarity of participants' experiences, I expect that many more participants came out first with an affinity as well. Recall that, as a part of my research methodology, I did not solicit any specific information regarding this form of coming out. Follow up interviews with the entire sample in this study may enable me to learn more about the prevalence and utility of coming out with affinity.

While analyzing the data related to affinities, I found myself pondering the methodological impact of these findings. A majority of social research, particularly survey research, relies on the assumption that people maintain concrete identities—this assumption is apparent in the commonness of "boxed" identity choices on most surveys for race, gender, sexuality, etc. From demographic questions related to sexual orientation to any number of other survey items, we often assume that participants or respondents can be categorized (and "boxed") according to their sexual orientation. Rarely do surveys allow respondents to speak of affinities or even affirm one of the progressive identities discussed in this chapter. Consider, for example, research on intimate partner violence (IPV). Only recently have studies on IPV included a focus on IPV within the LGBTQ community. Even still, survey items are undoubtedly written with the intent of differentiating patterns of violence among different populations (bisexuals versus heterosexuals, etc.). Based on the prevalence of progressive identities and the number of people who affirm an affinity rather than a prescribed identity, a large segment of the queer population can go missed in these analyses. In order to gain a fuller picture of how populations that are not explicitly heterosexual are impacted by IPV, or any other social issue, survey instruments and qualitative interviews must contain questions that allow people to describe themselves according to their sexual affinities (e.g., liking members of the same sex) as well as more concrete identities.

The differentiation between sexual identity and sexual affinity also brings to light another issue: our current language is inadequate for describing people's lived experiences related to sexuality. "Sexual identity" and "sexual orientation" are often used to refer to a static, fixed identity (i.e., "I am _____."). These two terms are also frequently used interchangeably, and scholars have differing opinions as to which concept is more fixed. But neither term is adequate for simply discussing individuals' attractions toward other people without presupposing that their identities align with such attractions. Having an affinity for members of the same sex predates the formation of an LGBQ identity, so the concept of "sexual affinity" is a more adequate way to refer to attractions without speaking of identity. This quandary over language may remain unresolved until society advocates an understanding that sexuality is not really a fixed "thing"—no matter how hard we try to treat it as such. Evidence from the current study suggests that sexuality is surprisingly fluid (both in-the-moment and across time), and sexuality would be perhaps even more fluid were social conventions to lighten up on the insistence that all people maintain a singular, concrete sexual identity.

It is becoming increasingly common for queer youth to come out multiple times to the same people and even themselves. This trend serves as perhaps the sharpest indication that sexuality remains quite fluid for most people. Numerous participants cited moving through a series of identities (or affinities) prior to landing on the current sexuality with which they identity. Some participants even suggested that their current sexuality may or may not be their final sexuality (a few even suggested that the fluidity of sexuality means that there is no such thing as a concrete sexual identity). The notion that sexual identities are not so straight-forward and therefore far from fixed was conveyed across many interviews. Granted, this study cannot be generalized to the entire U.S. LGBQ population.

Although there exists a great deal of variability among the 30 participants in this study, it is clear that many people still buy into the either/or dichotomy that permeates language and discourse in modern Western societies. Looking back on Chapter 3, many participants who used bisexuality as a transitional identity retain the current belief that there are really only two "true" sexualities (gay and straight). These individuals mirror an unfortunate truth shared among broader society—

sexualities that are in the middle of the spectrum (so to speak) are not legitimated as true identities. They are seen as rest stops on the way to an eventual gay identity. Evidence of this cultural belief can be seen in the extreme levels of biphobia that exist across contemporary society, even within the LGBTQ community. There is one related item of which I do not currently have much evidence, but I will ascertain in the near future. None of the participants in the current study identified as bisexual at the time of their interview. Considering how statistically prevalent bisexuality is in the United States I found myself wondering if youth today who would have identified as bisexual in decades past are instead choosing to identify as pansexual, fluid, or "not identified" simply because they do not view sex or gender as dichotomous categories. Or, as Eden demonstrated, some people may have moved away from bisexual identities in order to avoid bi-phobic stereotypes. Perhaps some of the individuals who expressed progressive identities to me are likely to check the box for "bisexual" on a survey instrument simply because, of the available choices, it is the option that most closely aligns with their sexuality. This is mere conjecture at this point, but a noteworthy idea to contemplate nonetheless.

In reflecting on my interviews with many other participants it appears that contemporary teens and young adults are less concerned with extraneous cultural expectations about sexuality. In my own encounters with youth groups in Central Florida, I have come to see that youth who assert that they are allies of the LGBTQ community are also likely to identify as pansexual or fluid (even though many of them have dating histories that include only members of the other sex). In these cases it appears that having a progressive view of gender and sexuality trumps any trends seen within an individual's dating history that would seem to indicate otherwise. My general sense is that the entire trajectory of forming and maintaining sexual identities is going through a major transformation in the U.S. and that our general cultural rhetoric on sexuality will shift drastically over the next 10-20 years. This assertion is supported by the proliferation of progressive identities that was discussed and conveyed by numerous participants. In fact, many participants explained to me the meanings of other identities of which are far from common. For example, Adam had friends who referred to themselves as "hetero-flexible." Hetero-flexible was explained to me as meaning "I'm straight, but shit happens." This identity, as well as many others, was left out of the discussion above since they were not identities that any of my participants attached to their own sexualities. The degree to which the acronym GLB has grown into LGBTQQIAFPP (and so on) demonstrates that new sexual identities are emerging which enable queer youth to more precisely identify and share their sexualities with other people.

A great deal of social research on issues faced by the LGBTQ community is aimed at advocating for education or the outright prevention of negative outcomes facing LGBTQ persons. Education and prevention programs (on topics such as bullying, IPV, and safe sex practices) are often directed toward youth populations, and younger people are less likely to have concrete sexual identities. Among the participants in this study who came out first as "liking boys/girls," all nine indicated doing so at a young age, most notably in their teens. At the time that they came out as "liking girls/boys" these individuals would have been unlikely to identify themselves as gay, lesbian, bisexual, etc. Still, this group is of import to any applied effort or research directed at limiting negative outcomes or advancing social justice for the queer communities. In addition to those who come out with affinity, more and more youth are choosing to attach their sexuality to the progressive identities such as pansexual or queer, both of which are often left out of rigid research designs. By focusing on affinity as well as identity in our research, we can work to learn more about populations of people who may otherwise be missed.

---

[1] "Sexual identity" and "sexual orientation" are terms that are often used interchangeably. However, they both assume a more fixed pattern of attraction toward certain categories or groups of people. "Affinity," on the other hand, is a more fluid concept that is centered on expressing to whom an individual may be attracted without ascribing or altering one's sexual identity. For the participants in this study, affinities were often expressed prior to the development of a more concrete sexual identity.

5

Gender (Non)Conformity

I have to come out more often than most because, uh, I don't, I'm not the stereotypical lesbian. When I, myself, think "oh, that girl's gay," she usually has short hair, maybe spiked, wears guys clothes—you can usually tell that she's either gay, gay accepting, transgendered, something, or very, very tomboyish, but usually the case is "oh yeah, she's probably gay."

~ Rachel

Rachel explains that she is not the "stereotypical lesbian." It's probably safe to assume that most people do not view themselves as a social stereotype. What does a stereotypical lesbian look like anyway? The common response to this question can be found in Rachel's quote—short hair, guys clothes, etc. In other words, being stereotypically gay largely means being a gender non-conformist (e.g., a masculine woman or a feminine man). Rachel was not alone in her discussion of stereotypes that are tied to sexuality. The majority of participants in this study made some reference to a "stereotypical" person of their own sexuality, and these references were used almost exclusively as a way to distance themselves from such "gay stereotypes." Stereotypes associated with sexuality are still quite pervasive in contemporary society. Despite the existence of research indicating that gender boundaries are becoming increasingly malleable (McCormack and Anderson 2010), recent research maintains that gender non-conformity is still the stereotypical mechanism used by many people who believe they can determine another person's sexuality (Blashill and Powlishta 2009; Rieger et al. 2010).

A great many of the assumptions we make about other people are predicated on their gender presentation. All too often people assume that that someone with a feminine gender presentation is attracted to men, while someone with a masculine gender presentation is attracted to women. In fact, this assumption is at the root of dualistic thinking surrounding matters of sex, gender, and sexuality. How then might people's gender presentation affect their coming out? How might coming out differ, for example, for a feminine lesbian as opposed to a lesbian with a more masculine gender presentation? Based on data from this study, it is apparent that the experiences of individuals who engage in coming out vary substantially depending on their gender presentation. A central concern here is whether gender conformity (e.g., a feminine female) or non-conformity (e.g., a masculine female) makes coming out a more difficult, arduous engagement.

Gender conformity refers to meeting the common social expectation that "sex = gender" (that is, "female + feminine" and "male + masculine"). By default, gender non-conformity is any relationship between sex and gender that does not align with this social expectation. For most Americans gender non-conformity refers more specifically to a masculine female or a feminine male. In contemporary U.S. culture, people commonly assume that gender non-conformists are gay. Younger people are more likely to experience this "assumed gayness" which is gradually confirmed without any explicit disclosure (Grierson and Smith 2005). In order to understand the common social expectation that men should be masculine and women should be feminine it is essential to understand the dualistic model with which most people perceive of sex, gender, and sexuality.

Figure 5.1 - The Gender Box Structure (Crawley et al. 2008)

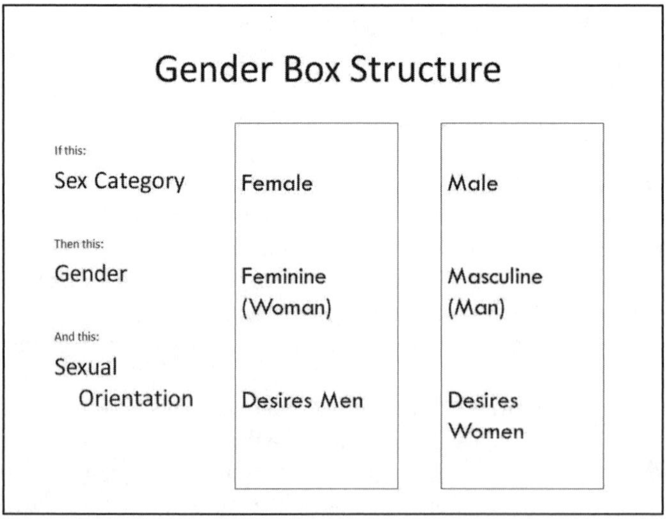

Gender Box Structure		
If this:		
Sex Category	Female	Male
Then this:		
Gender	Feminine (Woman)	Masculine (Man)
And this:		
Sexual Orientation	Desires Men	Desires Women

Traditionally, Western dualistic thought has dictated that we categorize people into one of two boxes in terms of sex category (female/male), gender (feminine/masculine), and sexual orientation (desires men/desires women) (Garfinkel 1967). The Gender Box Structure, detailed by Crawley, Foley, and Sheehan (2008) provides perhaps the clearest visual of our dualistic thinking on these three traits.

Crawley et al. (2008) built upon the work of scholars such as Lorber (1994) and Lucal (1999) in order to create their Gender Box Structure. As shown in Figure 5.1, this model shows how sex category, gender, and sexual orientation are fused. By "fused" I mean that we believe that to know someone's sex category is to know her gender and sexual orientation as well. At least this is our expectation. It is essential then to consider the interrelatedness of sex category, gender, and sexuality when analyzing experiences related to coming out.

Figure 5.2 - Heteronormative Assumptions of Sex, Gender, & Sexuality

Gender Box Structure

If this:	S E Q U E N T I A L		2 Mutually Exclusive Sets of Choices		S E Q U E N T I A L
Sex Category		Female		Male	
Then this:					
Gender		Feminine (Woman)	Zero Overlap	Masculine (Man)	
And this:					
Sexual Orientation		Desires Men		Desires Women	

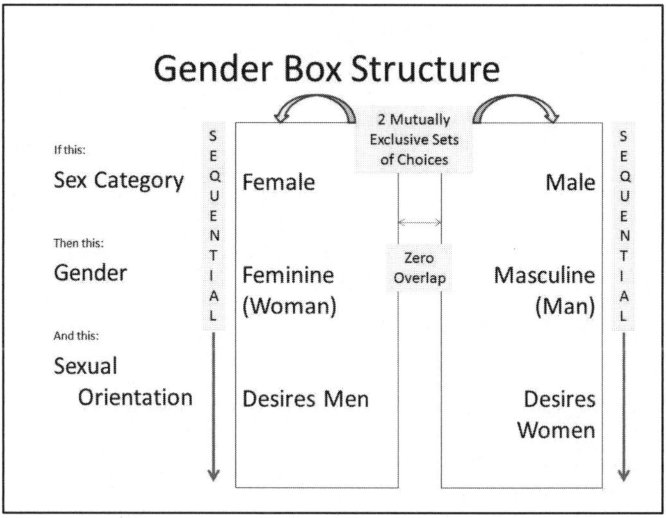

The equation of "sex = gender = sexuality" embodies heteronormative assumptions regarding sexuality. As Figure 5.2 details, everyone presumably falls into two, mutually exclusive categories—hence the gap between the two categories in this model. Society presupposes that males are masculine and desire women while females are feminine and desire men. We are held accountable concurrently on all three levels, and if any one level is called into question, so are the other two. So a male who desires men or a female who desires women both challenge our dualistic ideology—hence the cultural expectation to come out to others. In reality many people challenge traditional expectations (i.e., sex category ≠ gender ≠ sexuality) (Lucal 2008). So, how might gender conformity or non-conformity alter the coming out process?

Data from the interviews in this study indicate that experiences with coming out vary depending on one's gender presentation. This was particularly evident in my interactions with female participants. Figure 5.3 provides a visual example of gender conformity versus gender non-conformity among gay or lesbian women.

Figure 5.3 - Gender (Non)Conformity and Same-sex Attractions

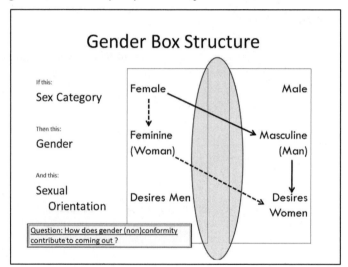

The dashed arrows represent a female who is feminine, which matches the heteronormative assumption that "sex = gender." The solid arrows represent a female who is masculine, and therefore runs counter to the "sex = gender" assumption. Both of these individuals are attracted to women, but their gender presentation is vastly different and so is their coming out. The central question in this chapter involves discerning how these two groups of people differ in their coming out. Does a gender conformist—who seemingly makes it further down the box of social expectations before crossing over—experience fewer difficulties coming out? Or does the gender non-conformist, who communicates "difference" more readily, experience fewer difficulties? I should note that a few individuals in this study present a more neutral and sometimes androgynous gender presentation. Neutrality or androgyny (both of which fall within the shaded bubble of Figure 5.3) is another form of gender non-conformity in that it still defies the common cultural expectation that females are explicitly feminine and males are explicitly masculine.

Gender Presentation & Coming Out

Among LGBQ persons who engage in coming out, gender presentation (whether conforming or non-conforming) presents unique challenges to the entire endeavor. The most frequently cited challenge associated with gender conformity is that, as Athena put it, a gender conformist does not "look gay." Social commentary and political correctness are quick to emphasize the danger in saying that gayness is sometimes physically identifiable. But the participants in this study very frequently spoke of such a thing. Looking or appearing gay was almost entirely related to *not* meeting the social expectation that "sex = gender." In other words, "visible gayness" is a matter of gender non-conformity. Ram, a gay male who is decidedly masculine in his presentation, is quick to point out that "it's a matter of how 'in your face' kind of gay you are . . . I don't really wear it on my sleeve." To Ram wearing it [his "gayness"] on his sleeve would be tantamount to appearing gay via gender non-conformity—that is, appearing feminine in some way. Participants who do not feel that they "look gay" often provide an example of a friend or a peer who does look gay in order to support their claims. As Ram continues,

> So, one of my friends, who is also my fraternity brother, he is just . . . you can't help him, he's twinklishous and he's tiny and he just wears these like deep V's that come down to here, so he can't help it.

Ram contends that his friend "can't help" but be assumed gay based on his appearance. To Ram "looking gay" has to do with attire, size, and as he later points out, speech and mannerisms. All of these characteristics challenge gender conventions, and, in the case of Ram's friend, make him appear to be challenging the whole "male = masculine" assumption, thereby leading others to visibly question his sexuality. But, the concern here is to ascertain how the coming out experiences of gender conformists like Ram, or gender non-conformists like his friend, might vary based on their gender presentation.

For the most part participants communicated that gender conformity makes for a less difficult coming out process. The lessened degree of difficulty deals primarily with the opinion that, on a daily basis, acquaintances and passers-by perceive them to be heterosexual. In the case of participants like Ram, there is an expressed sense of accomplishment in passing. "I think I take pride in the fact that when I do come out people are like 'oh, I had no idea.'" His sex category aligns with his assumed gender, thereby preventing outsiders from visibly questioning his sexuality. The idea that people expect gender presentation to tell us something about another person's sexuality is essentially rooted in broad social stereotypes.

In order to maintain a dualistic model of categorization, people often typify what it means to be this or that (e.g., masculine or feminine, gay or straight, black or white). Throughout the interviews in this study, the reality of LGBQ stereotypes was constantly looming in the background of conversation. Occasionally, the discussion of stereotypes entered the forefront of conversation. Lee, Renee, Ruby, Ram, Athena, Rachel, Kyle, and Arielle all made direct references to the stereotypical gay person or the stereotypical lesbian and whether or not they personally fit the stereotype. As was the case across this study, participants offered up little information about what comprised the "stereotypical gay person," except to say that gender presentation has a lot to do with such stereotypes. Stereotypes were more often discussed purely to convey that they (the individuals I interviewed) *did not see themselves as the stereotypical LGBQ person*. Lee demonstrated this very point in explaining how his coming out has been "fairly uneventful."

> There's my experience, where I fit this, I didn't, not that I fit the straight stereotype, but I didn't, I'm not, I don't fit the gay stereotype . . . people are just like "oh, I didn't think you were gay," and I'm just like "well, I am, whatever."

Part of the explanation for his mundane experiences is that he is not often perceived to be gay based on his gender presentation. This was a common trend among other participants as well. For example, Renee does not see herself as the "stereotypical lesbian." And, she feels that she does not have to come out as often as a result.

> I don't think that people expect me to share it [her sexuality] . . . I don't know, if you just saw me walking down the street and you want to go by what a stereotypical lesbian looks like, I don't ever get placed into that category. And a lot of times when I do tell people, they look and me and they go "oh, my gosh, I would never be able to tell." And

then I'm like, "of course, because we all are supposed to look a certain way, right?"

I could sense the tone in Renee's voice about how ridiculous it is that people assume to know what a lesbian looks like. But, in reality, she does perceive that people approach her differently based on the assumption that she is straight. So Renee's feminine gender presentation (i.e., her gender conformity) makes coming out easier in the sense that she has to engage in coming out less often. She went on to explain how she felt more control over when her sexuality would be discussed (such as when she was with her girlfriend) and when it would not be mentioned. This general sentiment was shared among other participants, such as Ruby.

Ruby maintains a broad, open perception of both gender and sexuality. But, she is keenly aware of how much appearance plays into other people's assumptions regarding her sexuality. She engaged in a lengthy discussion about how her feminine appearance has prevented her from receiving much of a backlash over her queer sexuality. She also shares some revealing insight into why she identifies with a feminine gender presentation.

> I choose to dress in the feminine gender because that's what's comfortable for me. Maybe it's because every single Sunday since I was born I've worn a dress to church, maybe it's because my ears were pierced at age 1 and I was thrown into, like swaddled in pink, and that's just always the way it was in my family. I was assimilated into this gender, but *I just don't face anything because of my appearance*, and that's not the way for a lot of people who just identify more with the male sex or the male gender by dressing more as a male that, as females, face a LOT of resistance (emphasis added).

In Ruby's calculation, female-bodied persons who align themselves with a masculine presentation face a lot more resistance than she does and therefore engage in coming out more often and in more difficult circumstances. By appearing to challenge their assumed gender, masculine-presenting females have their sexual orientation more frequently called into question. Another participant, Hannah, expanded on Ruby's discussion on the effects of gender conformity on coming out.

Hannah spoke at length about her perception that coming out is less difficult for women who are more traditionally feminine in their gender presentation. She attributes her relative ease in coming out to her heightened femininity.

There is a difference between a girl who looks like a very straight girl—and I look like a very straight girl—coming out and saying I'm a homosexual, and somebody who maybe is a little more awkward on the outside, you know what I mean?

She expands on this train of thought further. But, rather than focusing on herself and her own experiences, her discussion of gender presentation and coming out centers more on the experiences of her female friends who present more masculine.

One of my close friends is more of a butch-looking lesbian, and when she came out it was harder for her because she was awkward. You could tell she was butch but her hair was long and kind of awkward looking, and it was harder for her.

Hannah's repeated use of the word "awkward" is interesting. Essentially, she is stating that her friend's sex category does not align with heteronormative expectations of gender presentation (i.e., female ≠ feminine). But, hidden within Hannah's wording there is also a sense that gender non-conformity may be seen as challenging homonormativity as well. In recent years there has been increasing dialog about how large segments of the LGBQ community are adopting the same gendered expectations commonly associated with heteronormativity (Duggan 2002). In her summation, "awkward" appears to be synonymous with challenging others' expectations of sex and gender. Since the expectation of "sex = gender" is not met, her friend's sexuality is more frequently called into question as well. As a result, Hannah sees coming out as a more manageable process for females who present feminine—someone like her.

Hannah's logic is partially rooted in her opinions of her friends and their experiences, but another participant, Kyle, confirms the same trend from the opposite end of the spectrum. Kyle is oftentimes assumed to be gay, and this assumption is based on her gender presentation. "If it's people I'm comfortable with, I'm like 'yeah, I'm gay.' A lot of people just can *tell* I'm gay." Kyle typically keeps her hair short and dresses in baggy clothes, some of which are hand-me-downs from her older brother. She goes on to give an example of her interactions with her peers that led her to the conclusion that she is assumed gay.

If I get comfortable with someone, and they start talking about "oh, my boyfriend did this," or "oh, my girlfriend . . ." then eventually it might come to "oh, are you dating anyone Kyle," and I'll just be like "yes, I'm dating a girl." And, a lot of them will be like "we could kind of tell," and I'm like "ok, thanks." They're like "no, it's not that you're a stereotypical lesbian, it's just that you kind of have that vibe thing going on."

Again, we see the mention of a "stereotypical lesbian." In Kyle's case, her seemingly masculine characteristics (coupled with a name that is typically masculine in the U.S.) have sometimes even led people to assume that she is a female-to-male transgender person. "A lot of girls in my classes thought I was a boy because my name was Kyle, I never spoke in class, I always wore baggy clothes . . ." Soon after, she emphasizes that she is "really girly," she just doesn't look that way. The end result is that Kyle's androgynous, and sometimes masculine, gender presentation has made for a tumultuous coming out process. In fact, the backlash she faced from appearing to defy gender expectations was greater than any reaction to her sexuality. This sort of phenomena will garner greater interest below.

So, all things being equal, it seems that gender conformity makes for a less tumultuous coming out process. But, there is another side to the topic of gender conformity and coming out. Although gender conformity may contribute to an individual having her sexuality questioned less often publicly, it may also make it more difficult to come out to those people closest to her. For example, Rachel recalls her high school years where she was first grappling with the disclosure of her sexuality to her friends and family. Initially she did not want to come out to other people as being gay because everyone who was out at her school was "obviously gay." There was nobody like her who was out—nobody who was more in line with traditional gender expectations.

> I didn't want to come out because there weren't any girls like me out there that people assumed, "oh, she's straight, she's got long hair, she wears girls clothes usually." Like, I would wear skate shoes, but people would usually assume I was a punk, so it was just, I felt like I was the only one like myself that's somewhere between, like, tomboy and femme, and so that's kind of what my high school's like. It's like everyone was either in the closet, or, like, obviously gay.

So, when Rachel does come out, she feels that she has to make a more concerted effort to do so due to her femininity. In her summation, women whose gender presentation does not label them as "stereotypical lesbians" have to come out more often as a result. Rachel is not assumed gay, so she must be more direct about coming out in order to get the point across.

> I actually feel like I have to come out more often than most because, uh, I don't, I'm not the stereotypical lesbian. Um I mean I'm not exactly very, very feminine but when I, myself, think "oh, that girl's gay," she usually has short hair, maybe spiked, wears guys clothes . . . you can usually tell that she's either gay, gay accepting, transgendered, something, or very, very tomboyish, but usually the case is "oh yeah, she's probably gay." And, with me, I just look like sort of a tomboyish, maybe a punk or musician, indie girl with long hair and pretty feminine, so I feel like I have to come out more than most people.

In contemporary society, we already operate under the assumption that everyone is straight until proven otherwise. This is why Rachel feels that her femininity forces her to come out more often than other women who present more masculine.

Self-Presentation as Coming Out

Our family members and close friends have known us longer than anyone, so they have spent the most time operating under an assumption that we are all straight. Consequently, a young woman whose gender presentation is decidedly feminine—and therefore conforms to traditional gender expectations—may find it more challenging to come out to her family. Rachel spoke briefly of this, but another participant, Renee, provides a perfect example of this interaction. Although she acknowledged above that her femininity has made for a smoother coming out process in general, it still provided an additional challenge to her coming out to her family. She perceives that her femininity kept her mom from acknowledging that she might be gay. In her summation, she didn't look gay, so any news of her being attracted to women would come out of nowhere. Eventually, Renee figured that dating and bringing home women with a more masculine presentation would ultimately communicate her sexuality to her mom.

> And I guess my mom was pretty, like, just had no idea. She's like [oblivious] "I just told everyone you and [your girlfriend] were good friends." I'm like "couldn't you kind of tell with her?" Me, not so much, cuz I am pretty feminine, and I dress feminine and stuff like that, but she is tall, real short hair. She had wore, like, men's clothing and stuff like that. I don't want to stereotype, but it is what it is, and that is the world of lesbians.

Although Renee feels that her femininity made it harder for her mom to "realize" her daughter was a lesbian, she still sees her feminine presentation as easing the rest of the process—at least on the public side of things. In the end, Renee tried to utilize gender non-conformity (via her girlfriend's gender non-conformity) to appear more visibly gay and resultantly come out to her mom. So, she was operating under the same assumption held by many of the other participants: "gender non-conformity = assumed gayness." This technique of purposively utilizing gender non-conformity in order to visibly come out was employed to a greater degree by other participants as well. As Arielle describes:

> Sometimes you have to like announce it or come out with it because you can [otherwise] pass as straight because, like, sometimes I can look really, really gay *laughter* you know, like, well [today] I just kind of rolled out of bed and put the first thing on I saw but, um, sometimes I look really, really gay . . . I just look like a big 'ole dike.

Gay and lesbian persons sometimes purposively use appearance as a way to communicate sexual difference and achieve a sense of authenticity with a gay or lesbian identity (Hutson 2010). According to Hutson, gay and lesbian women are often encouraged to present as "butch" in order to appear authentically gay—but they are equally held accountable to their woman-ness and therefore called upon to express some form of femininity as well. Arielle walked this line quite well. Her periodic employment of a masculine gender presentation mirrored that of the Gay-Straight Alliance (GSA) Girls in Pascoe's (2007:152) seminal work on masculinity and sexuality in high school. This alternating appearance results in a destabilization of gender norms—Arielle is recognized as doing masculinity while not entirely parting from the feminine domain within which she largely resides. This double-bind is also emblematic of institutionalized oppression.

Gabrielle echoed Arielle's stance on presenting a more masculine appearance in order to appear more visibly gay. Upon first coming out she used her appearance as a way to generally and broadly come out. That is, she felt a sort of self-imposed disclosure imperative and therefore used her gender presentation to periodically allow others to infer her sexuality as gay.

> I definitely felt the need to tell everyone that I was gay, and I also felt the need to . . . when I first came out I was also a little bit dikier . . . I wore the big t-shirts and I was insecure about my body, but I was also a little bit dikier because I felt the need to show the world that I was a lesbian or that I liked women.

So, all three of these women at one point operated under the same assumption held by many of the other participants: "gender non-conformity = assumed gayness." But, these women perceived gender non-conformity as a way to simplify the coming out process. Other participants, whom we discussed prior, felt that gender non-conformity makes coming out more difficult. It is apparent then that coming out is not strictly more difficult for either gender conformists or non-conformists. Gender is a very personal matter, as is coming out, and this is most evident among those participants who do not present explicitly feminine or masculine.

In the Middle

As is the case with most people, many LGBQ persons do not exclusively present feminine or masculine. Oftentimes, individuals demonstrate some traits that are deemed more traditionally in line with one gender while concurrently showcasing traits considered reminiscent of the other gender. Regardless, people are still arbitrarily placed by others into one of two gender categories: masculine or feminine. However, an individual's gender presentation may shift from day-to-day, or situation-to-situation. In other words, few people are 100% masculine or 100% feminine all the time, so an individual's relative alignment with gender conformity or gender non-conformity is fluid. Consider Eden, who dresses in the feminine gender, and is oftentimes assumed to be heterosexual purely based on her gender presentation.

> I feel a lot of times, I'm going to the grocery store or something like that, and I say because I dress in the female gender, people will never know I'm gay. So, to them, they could care less . . . they could totally care less. They will never know I'm gay. They live their life, there are no gays in this world, and they're happy as clams.

Yet, Eden is often seen in public with her girlfriend who dresses in the masculine gender. In such circumstances her femininity is overridden by her accompaniment with another female who appears to be a masculine intimate partner. And she finds herself engaging in coming out in new and unusual circumstances.

> But, maybe if they see me dressed as the female gender, and with my girlfriend dressed in the male gender, being a female, seeing her breasts underneath her clothing and us holding hands, then they feel like they might have to confront that situation either outwardly or inwardly, and reflect. People sometimes get really frustrated when

they see me dressed in my femininity and they want to know why I'm not a heterosexual. I would gladly set some time aside and say "that's ok that you don't understand, but now you're thinking about these things." I choose to dress in the feminine gender because that's what's comfortable for me.

Eden's experiences demonstrate how people are held accountable concurrently on all three levels (sex, gender, and sexuality), and if any one level is called into question, so are the other two. She is both a female and feminine, and therefore assumed to be attracted to men. But once people are provided with evidence to the contrary, her gender is called into question. Although sexual orientation is less about gender identity and more about for whom an individual has sexual or affectual attractions, it's relation to doing gender is very clear (Jackson 2006). Gender presentation informs many of the assumptions people make about others' sexual identities (Miller and Lucal 2009). People extract contextual cues from others' apparent sex category and gender presentation in order to determine their sexuality. So, what happens when people do not clearly align themselves with one gender or the other?

Like Eden, Carly often gets varied responses from other people on different occasions, and she finds herself disclosing her sexuality based on other people's reactions to her gender presentation. But, unlike Eden, the variety in Carly's experiences is based on variation in her own gender presentation, which is sometimes feminine and other times masculine.

I confuse people that I first meet because sometimes I dress very masculine and sometimes I dress very feminine so people sometimes get confused. I've had people where I'd been in a class for like a whole semester and then I'll say something, maybe about feminism or something, and then they'll ask me "wait, ok, so you're a feminist?" I'm like "yeah." "So, are you a lesbian?" "Well, yeah, kind of." And then it's like, "really because sometimes you wear dresses, and sometimes you wear bows, and sometimes you wear makeup, and I just, like, you know, I don't get it." People are just very confused, so sometimes there is that moment of me being like "yes, I guess I'm coming out to you right now to try to help you understand because you want to put me in a box, and you don't like that I confuse you."

The fact that Carly's gender, and therefore her sexuality, is challenged by other people leads her to engage in more frequent, and sometimes impromptu situational coming out moments. Again, the lack of consistent alignment with the feminine gender makes for a more tumultuous coming out process. The final conclusion drawn by Carly is in harmony with what Rachel was speaking of above. Those who do not appear "obviously queer" may find additional difficulty coming out since people are taken aback by the apparent incongruity of their gender and sexual orientation.

> People feel like they need to know that about you [your sexuality] for whatever reason because you're not "normal" or whatever. And, so, yeah, I feel that people expect you, and that's especially true for people who are not, like, very obviously queer, you know, because there's a lot of people who you look at them and you wouldn't say "oh, they're definitely not straight," and, but it's the people that are more confusing like if I wear a dress but I don't tell you that I'm queer, like, I'm sorry that I tricked you, I'm not trying to trick anyone, but people expect that I guess.

Carly perceives that other people may feel "tricked" by being confronted with an apparent incongruity between her gender and sexuality. People see femininity, and then expect that the she—or any other individual who exhibits femininity—is attracted to men.

This leads into the discussion of Veronica and Nathan who, like Carly, see their gender presentation as somewhere in the middle, or rather part of a continuum between extreme femininity and extreme masculinity. As Veronica puts it, "I'm kind of on the fence, like the way I look and dress. You know, I wear makeup, I consider myself feminine—I'm not totally femme . . . I've always been a tomboy, and I'm kind of on the fence, I've always been neutral." Veronica's experiences resemble those of Carly in that people sometimes recognize her as not exclusively aligning with the feminine gender expectations that they impose upon her. Nathan's intermediate gender expression is related more to "how gay" he believes he comes off. "I'm not a flamboyant flamer, but I also feel that I don't try to cover it up, I just . . . it is ME." Nathan is ardently aware that his lack of hegemonic masculinity leads to his sexuality being questioned. This results in him more often coming out publicly.

> I think for a lot of people it is very easy to tell if I am [gay]. So, even then, I feel like that is almost a form of coming out because, even if they are making assumptions, which usually leads to them asking questions, them asking a friend "hey, is Nathan gay," type thing . . .

Some participants, as well as some scholars, contend that "assumed gayness" creates an environment in which an individual does not have to truly "come out." But, in Nathan's purview, assumed gayness (the result of his gender non-conformity) still leads to new forms of coming out. Although he is not setting out to disclose his sexuality other people, he ends up engaged in coming out nonetheless—oftentimes simply to confirm other people's assumptions. So the social environment dictates that coming out is still relevant.

To be clear, most participants in this study do not personally align themselves with only femininity or only masculinity. Nonetheless, each participant was aware that other people, and society in general, will force them into one box or the other. This was demonstrated at the conclusion of each interview when I asked the participants to identify their gender. With the exception of Ruby, every single participant chose one of our two expected choices (i.e., woman or man). Remember, anything in the middle is still seen as running counter to our general, heteronormative expectations of gender, and therefore sexuality. As the interviews progressed, participants frequently clarified that their gender is much more complex than simply feminine or masculine—woman or man.

Parental Resistance to Gender Non-Conformity

Individuals often experience a great deal of anxiety during the formation and maintenance of an LGBQ identity. As a central element in this process, coming out naturally involves feelings of anxiety as well. For many people, such anxiety reaches its climax during the disclosure of one's sexual identity to close friends and family. After all, there is more at stake in the relationships we have with our inner circle than with anyone else. Although fear is rooted in expectations of rejection, many LGBQ persons are surprised to find that family members and close friends are more accepting and affirming than was originally predicted. Ironically, even parents often report being much more accepting than their LGBQ children anticipated (Savin-Williams & Dube 1998). To the surprise of many of the participants in this study, it was not so much their sexuality, but rather their gender presentation that family and close friends were most concerned about.

Sexuality is one of those unseen characteristics of our lives. More times than not, we can physically identify one another on the basis of race or age, but sexual orientation is a whole different arena. Gender, on the other hand, is much more visually apparent than sexuality. Gender is something that is done, something that is achieved, and it is about identity as well as expression. But, gender is also something that gets treated by much of the general population as innate, natural, and essentially different depending on one's sex category. From birth, or perhaps even earlier, we are inundated with gendered expectations. Prompted by society at large, our families socialize us from day one to be a tough little boy, or a polite little girl, and so on. But, gender is not only about behavior, it is also about physical expression. Gender materializes in our clothing, hair styles, grooming habits, and myriad other attributes and characteristics.

Given the essentialized treatment of gender, it should come as no real shock that family and friends can be very resistant to any inkling of gender non-conformity. Many participants recall being completely blindsided by their family's reaction to their gender presentation, not their sexual orientation, upon coming out. Ari jokingly quipped, "My parents find more of a problem with me not shaving my legs than with me being gay {chuckle}. So, they have very strict gender roles . . . they're Latino, so, but you know, so it came out alright." In many cases, gender non-conformity is the issue more so than sexual orientation. This is particularly true among families with traditional, conservative views of gender—like Ari's family. Ari began to notice hints of gender resistance emanating from her family well before she came out to them as a lesbian. Like so many young women, Ari developed body image issues as a result of lofty social expectations and unrealistic media imagery bathed in emphasized femininity. Wearing a large shirt or baggie pants gave her a sense of comfort, but this style of dress was not well received by her family.

As Ari's sexuality developed and she realized that she "liked girls," she found herself increasingly comfortable in clothing that was not traditionally associated with young women. Her gender presentation became intimately tied to her sexuality and her sense of expression. She recalls a specific interaction between her and her mom in which it became apparent to her that gender presentation was going to continue to be an issue.

> So we went to Express and I was looking at the men's section, and I saw this really nice tie that I wanted, and I showed it to my mom, and she just kind of did a double-take and she's like "why do you want to wear that? That's a man's tie," and I'm like "Because. I think it's really cute and I think I'd totally rock this." And, we just got into this argument about the tie in the middle of the store, you know, which the tie to me meant so much more than that but clearly she couldn't understand why and it's because, you know, she didn't know [that I am a lesbian]."

This conversation ultimately became the catalyst for her telling her mom and dad that she is attracted to women. Even as her interest in the same sex developed into a more concrete lesbian identity, she continued to face resistance on account of her gender presentation. And this is all after her family affirmed her sexuality. Issues over gender presentation continued well after coming out in much the same way for another participant, Gabrielle. Gabrielle recollects how it took quite a while for her mom to accept her being gay, and how her mom's reluctance was rooted in the fear that her daughter would begin to present more masculine.

> [On coming out] . . . it took two years for her to be cool with it. I think her biggest fear was the fact that she was afraid I was going to get really dikey, and cut my hair, you know, but what if I did? I think she would love me regardless. I think that's just something that she is thankful that I'm not.

Gabrielle's gender presentation is decidedly feminine, and she credits much of her family's acceptance of her sexuality to the fact that she does not defy traditional gender expectations. In my later discussions with Gabrielle she reiterated part of the point I made above about the visibility of gender. Parents who are still not entirely accepting of their child's sexuality may take more issue with gender presentation because, consistent with stereotypical images of gay men and lesbians, gender non-conformity comes to be seen as the physical manifestation of gayness. So, in her reaction, Gabrielle's mom essentially communicates a sense of "I'm ok with you being gay, but I don't want you to show it off to everyone else in the way you look."

Objections to gender non-conformity came not only from parents, but also from extended family and close friends. For example, Kyle recalls the reactions of her extended family to her coming out.

> The rest of the family is like "yeah, that's cool [her being gay]" . . . my grandpa is fine with it too—his wife was a little iffy, but my grandpa loves my girlfriend too, so it's all good. He had met my *ex*-girlfriend and he was like "I'm glad you got rid of her, she looked weird," and I was like [sarcastically] "thanks Grandpa, that's awesome," and he was like "well, she looked like a little boy."

Again, family members have more of a problem with gender non-conformity than sexual orientation. Objections to Kyle's gender presentation went well outside the home. She recalls her gender, not her sexuality, being the focus of a great deal of harassment and ridicule at school.

> . . . harassment came later [after coming out], or well, harassment came before also because I was pretty androgynous, like younger. I would cut my hair really short and I would wear boy's clothing, and it's really just because that's what I was comfortable in, and so in my 9th grade year a lot of girls in my classes thought I was a boy because my name was Kyle, I never spoke in class, I always wore baggy clothes.

She later goes on to say that she is actually quite "girly," she just doesn't look that way. Harassment over her gender presentation forced her hand at coming out on numerous occasions. It's almost as if her peers were satisfied to hear that Kyle was gay because it clarified her androgynous and sometimes masculine gender presentation. In a sense, her friends could then attribute her gender non-conformity to her lesbianness, and keep the traditional notions of "sex = gender" intact. But, the fact remains that Kyle's gender presentation has made for some exceedingly difficult experiences associated with coming out.

Attractiveness and Coming Out

People who are considered "classically attractive" face some distinctive circumstances in terms of coming out. As Hannah put it, "people seem to, in this society, accept, let's say pretty people, more than they would somebody who wasn't as physically attractive." There is plenty of literature to support the notion there is a sense of privilege that comes along with being classically attractive. We already saw how parents sometimes seem to be more concerned about their child's gender conformity than their child's sexuality. In the U.S., classical attractiveness is generally rooted in gender conformity, and in many cases gender conformity to the nth degree. Hegemonic masculinity and emphasized femininity are pervasive social forces that define much of our social interaction. Based on my interactions with the participants in this study, attractiveness can definitely affect coming out—particularly for young women. But, outside of immediate family, attractiveness seems to serve as a burden much more than a privilege.

Throughout the interviews attractiveness was mentioned only by the women in this study. In most cases, women discussed how their attractiveness led to many uncomfortable encounters with male friends and acquaintances. Five of the participants spoke specifically of how coming out was made more difficult by straight men finding them attractive and making advances toward them. Rachel had a variety of such experiences, particularly when she tried to befriend straight men.

> It's happened a lot of times where I'll meet a guy and I'm like "oh, he's a cool guy, I wanna be friends with him," and then he'll start hitting on me, and then he'll start wanting to hang out more and then he'll start acting more, like, flirty, and then I'm like "hey, I'm sorry, I'm gay, so . . . ."

Rachel, like the other women who spoke of such encounters, disclosed her sexuality in an effort to avoid further advances. "Guys stand and start talking to me and hitting on me, and I feel like I have to come out so they'll stop." One would think that coming out would discourage further advances from heterosexual men, but it is rarely that simple.

Gabrielle said that she always comes out as a lesbian when men flirt with her, but it does not always help her cause. "I feel comfortable just saying that I'm a lesbian because I know that guys aren't . . . well, that's not necessarily true . . . actually, guys might hit on me even more because of it." Gabrielle acknowledged the common heterosexual male fantasy of being with two women simultaneously as the source of the perseverance exhibited by men who come-on to her. Athena articulated this very issue and how it makes little sense to her. "Straight men find that attractive, two women together, but why would they want to watch two women that don't want them?" Nonetheless, Gabrielle does often come out to men that flirt with her in an attempt to cast them off.

> I don't tell everyone that I'm gay, but at least, a lot of guys end up hitting on me, so in that respect, you know, I end up going "you know, I'm gay," but I could've just been like "I'm not interested," but I guess maybe to get them off my chest, I just say that I'm gay and then they they're like "ok," or then they try harder. There's a reason I don't go to straight bars.

Veronica has had numerous encounters which mirror what Rachel and Gabrielle are talking about. Her experiences emphasize how, among a group of straight men, lesbians may even be treated as a spectacle. After all, the male gaze is an oppressive force that is not bound by the target's sexual orientation.

> . . . your average Joe at a party that your straight roommate throws, you know, they don't know a lot about it, and you become a spectacle, especially as a lesbian, and a lesbian who knows she's not ugly, and

gets a lot of responses and has to explain herself, you become a spectacle and you become a sexual spectacle when you just want to be treated normally.

So, there are some circumstances where coming out may simply foster more unwanted advances. But, for the most part, the women in this study preferred to be "open and honest." Coming out at least allowed them to take comfort in knowing that they did not lead anyone on, nor did they allow their sexuality to be ignored.

The relationship between attractiveness and coming out still goes one step further. Just as Carly spoke about people feeling tricked when she came out to her peers, men may react as if they were tricked if attractive women "hide" their true sexuality, or rather, their disinterest in men. Michelle has had many run-ins with men that ended in this sort of outcome.

> A lot of people, you know, if you don't come out, then they get mad, like, say if you thought I was attractive and I don't come out to you, then they get mad. Like, I had that happen a lot in the military. Like, they expect, "ok, this is who I am," you know, so that they don't waste their time type thing.

Michelle's experiences are rooted not only in her gender presentation and attractiveness, but also the social environment in which the events she is discussing take place. She is interacting with men in a military setting in which the assumption of straightness is even greater than in typical social settings. Masculinity is pervasive in the military, and Michelle's experiences took place during the enforcement of Don't Ask, Don't Tell. So although her male colleagues apparently preferred to know that she was gay, the social structure prevented her from disclosing her sexuality except with a few confidants.

Classical attractiveness definitely poses some unique challenges to coming out among LGBQ women. Rachel summarizes the main issues with men finding her attractive in a single statement. "I feel like in some ways I do have to come out a lot and just have to disclose that to people because otherwise they're just not going to get it from looking at me and talking to me." Based on common stereotypes, Rachel's femininity does not physically communicate her sexuality. Men find Rachel's feminine gender expression attractive. She is compelled to overcompensate and ward off male sexual advances by coming out as gay. In accordance with our common social expectation that "sex = gender = sexuality," her gender conformity makes coming out a more arduous process.

Discussion and Conclusion

The influence of gender presentation on coming out varies from person to person. For some people gender conformity lightens the load for coming out broadly because many acquaintances and peers assume that they are straight. For other people, gender conformity makes coming out more difficult because they have to make a more concerted effort to come out to others—again, because other people assume them to be straight based on their gender presentation. Gender conformity does, however, seem to be more well-received by family members who are still reluctant to affirm their child's sexuality. After reflecting on the way in which family members and friends react to gender non-conformity, it is apparent that males who present more feminine and females who present more masculine often face additional difficulties in coming out. But, as Gabrielle and Renee pointed out, gender non-conformity may also serve the purpose of communicating to others more broadly that one is not heterosexual (at least based on the assumption that "gender non-conformity = assumed gayness").

Individual variation in the perceived effects of gender conformity on coming out may have to do with what coming out means to each individual. For those who see coming out as a matter of full disclosure—that is, telling any and every one—gender non-conformity may aid the cause. However, those individuals who see coming out as being more about disclosing their sexuality to close family and friends may find gender conformity to ease the difficulty. Of course, these last few statements are based in the assumption that one's gender presentation is used purposively to physically communicate one's sexuality. And, as demonstrated by Eden and Ruby, in most cases our gender expression is rooted in so much more. Gender is a matter of what makes us comfortable as individuals, and it is also a form of play which we use to attract potential partners. Nevertheless, gender presentation can and often does have an effect on coming out.

One element of gender conformity that was not previously discussed is its effect on coming out to other people within the LGBQ community. Without much data on this, I was in no position to develop much of a discussion about it. But, one participant, Alex, spoke of her anxiety about coming out to her LGBQ peers—wondering how they would receive her. In her purview, feminine females are favored in the gay community the same way as in society at large. When she was first coming out, Alex modeled herself on her friend Natty "because she was pretty, she was feminine, which in the gay community is sometimes just as important as being pretty." Alex hits on the influence of both gender conformity and attractiveness. Most of the discussion throughout this chapter centered on the discussion of gender presentation as it relates to heteronormativity, but Alex's statement beckons further research into gender presentation, attractiveness, and homonormativity.

As scholars Lucal (1999) and Crawley et al. (2008) emphasize, in our heteronormative society, to have one's gender questioned is to have one's sexuality questioned, and vice versa. A woman whose femininity is called into question will quickly find that her sexuality is suspect as a result, and the same trend holds true for men. At the same time, those individuals whose gender is not called into question still face myriad challenges in the formation and maintenance of their sexual identity. Coming out therefore often differs based on whether our gender falls in line with traditional expectations or not.

6

Not a Process, But a Career

It's a constant process. It's something that people ask you "oh, do you have a girlfriend?" or something like that. It's a constant process, it's not something that you do and you finish, it's something you do for life.

~ Brandon

Twenty years ago renowned sexuality scholar Paula Rust (1993) asserted that coming out is not a simple linear, goal-oriented, developmental process. As is the case with most social phenomena, coming out is messy. The experiences associated with coming out are as numerous as the number of people who engage in coming out. Relatively little social research has investigated the temporal side of coming out. The common rhetoric is that coming out is a process filled with a series of linear "stages." But in analyzing recent research we see evidence of coming out as both a point-in-time event and a gradual process. More recently, researchers have begun to posit that coming out is an *unending* process (see Johnson's *My Revolving Closet Door* (2008) for a great example). In other words, coming out is less of a process and more of a *career*.

One of the more prevalent dimensions across all 30 interviews in this study was that of temporality. Participants had a great deal to say (both directly and contextually) about how long coming out takes and whether or not it ever truly ends. In most circumstances, participants spoke purely of their own experiences with coming out, and they made very few references to any general cultural trends. While speaking of their own personal experiences, participants anecdotally reiterated a few basic temporal elements to coming out. These can be categorized into three general groups explaining the duration and form that coming out may take: coming out as a point-in-time event, coming out as a gradual process, and coming out as a career. Most participants alluded to multiple temporal dimensions in their discussions of coming out, and there was substantial variability regarding which temporal elements seemed to be more central to the meaning of coming out. Despite participants alluding to the point-in-time and processional nature of coming out, the broader experiences shared by participants uncovered an enduring truth—coming out never really ends (or at least there is no clear end in sight).

Historically, most research on coming out has focused on coming out as a process—one which may be completed after a series of parameters have been met. These studies are typically written from a psychological perspective, most of which have been based around identifying "stages" of coming out. Research on the stages of coming out are generally aimed at identifying a standardized series of junctures that each individual purportedly moves through until one is figuratively "out" (Coleman 1982; Carrion and Lock 1997). Frequently cited stages include exploration and experimentation, meeting other LGBQ persons, coming out to oneself, telling family and friends, and publicly acknowledging one's sexual orientation (Cass 1979; Martin 1993). Models such as these, which end in the broad public sharing of one's sexuality, include a basic assumption that coming out is about full disclosure (a perspective that is challenge repeatedly throughout the current study). In addition to studies that focus on the process engaged by the individual coming out, some scholars have attempted to identify stages experienced by those people to whom an LGBQ person comes out—most notably family members (Ben-Ari 1995; Savin-Williams and Dube 1998).

Psychological models have their merit—hence why they are utilized by clinicians who work with the LGBQ community as well as ally training programs around the country. Those familiar with the Cass model of coming out may have even noticed similarities between the stages in the Cass model and the meanings ascribed to coming out by many of the participants in Chapter 2. One could make the argument that participant language mirrors many linear stage models simply because these models have become so pervasive that they have effectively entered the domain of popular culture thereby affecting the ways in which we view identity formation. This argument would explain the vast difference between participants' general views of coming out (which are more formulaic) and the individual experiences they shared with me (which are quite unique). Despite the loose connection between linear stage models and the participants in this study, my research challenges standardized models of coming out in a few major ways.

Psychological models of coming out often assume unidirectional movement through a series of stages until one ultimately achieves a level of sexuality-based self-actualization. Developmental psychologist Ritch Savin-Williams (2001) was one of the first social scientists to publicly dismiss the rigid coming out processes proposed by other developmental psychologists, and he is quick to point out how these models do not adequately characterize the lives of real people. They fail to recognize the unique circumstances faced by each person who engages in coming out. Other scholars in the social and behavioral sciences have also been critical of linear stage models. Eliason and Schope (2007) have suggested that our best alternative is to maintain some elements of stage models while still allowing identity formation to be a highly individual phenomenon. I should clarify that some stage models do allow for some variability—they may take into account that individuals can advance through certain stages only to revisit them again down the road. Still linear stage models still tend to assume that coming out will be completed. Is coming out really just a means to an end, or is it an endeavor that one continues to maneuver and manage throughout the life cycle—that is, is coming out a career?

The notion that coming out is a career is not an entirely new line of thinking. As far back as the 1970s, researchers began referring to sexual minorities as having to engage in a "homosexual career." Use of the catchall category of "homosexual" in that body of work predates the contemporary use of more appropriate labels for non-heterosexual identities (gay, lesbian, bisexual, queer, etc.). Kenneth Plummer (1975) was one of the first social scientists to refer to homosexuality as a static identity—one that would require an individual to engage in an enduring career. He also cleverly noted that homosexuality is a social construct utilized by the sexual majority in order to label and stigmatize a sexual minority—as assertion similar to those found in Katz's *The Invention of Heterosexuality* (2007). Plummer posited that gay men experience four different stages pertaining to their sexual orientation: sensitization, signification, coming out, and stabilization. Coming out only appears to be only a single element in the broader definition of Plummer's homosexual career. However, the other stages in his model closely mirror aspects of coming out as discussed by participants in this study. For example, Plummer's stage of "signification" refers to the self-acceptance of a gay identity—something that we now know to be central to (or even synonymous with) coming out rather than a mere precursor to coming out. He also recognized that not everyone experiences all of these contingencies, and that each individual will likely experience these stages in very different ways.

Plummer's work is mired by the fact that he frames homosexuality purely as a deviant career (as was popular at the time). Still, his recognition of sexual minorities as engaging in perpetual introspection, coming out, and stabilization (the management of an affirmed gay identity) is admirable given that his writings came around the same time that society was just reeling from the declassification of homosexuality as a psychological disorder (it was officially declassified by the APA in 1973, and this change was reflected in the DSM III). Three particular elements of Plummer's model shone through the narratives provided by participants in the current study: 1) coming out and the formation of a gay identity is a unique experience for each person, 2) coming out includes internal (self-affirmation) as well as external interactions, and 3) the maintenance of a non-heterosexual identity does not have a clear end—rather it is a career.

Recent research in the social sciences has continued to recognize coming out as a life-long progression (see Johnston and Jenkins' 2003 study of people coming out in mid-adulthood and Appleby's 2001 study of coming out among working-class gay and bisexual men). This chapter extends that line of conceptualization into the model of coming out as a career. All 30 participants in this study agreed that coming out is a transformative, ongoing endeavor. The meanings individuals attributed to coming out often alluded to an enduring quality of coming out, but participants spoke just as frequently about coming out as a point-in-time event (or series of point-in-time events) as well as a process. Prior to delving into the discussion of coming out as a career, we begin with participants' references to coming out as a point-in-time event and/or a gradual process

Coming out as a Point-in-Time Event and/or Gradual Process

Throughout my interviews, most participants engaged in conversation about how they came out to specific people (a parent, a best friend, or perhaps a coworker) during specific interactions. These instances highlight the meaning of coming out as a point-in-time event. As a point-in-time event, coming out is similar to "telling" as discussed in the Chapter 2. It serves the purpose of disclosing one's sexual orientation to an individual or a group in a single setting at a single moment. For example, when I questioned Ram about his coming out experience, he replied "I would say I never had *a* perfect coming out story with any one person (emphasis added)." Later on, he revisited this concept by indicating that he has "never had *a* smooth coming out." His use of the article "a" indicates coming out as a point-in-time event—or rather, a series of point-in-time events.

As was the case with every participant who indicated coming out as a point-in-time event, Ram also recognized coming out as a gradual, ongoing process (comprised of individual "outings"). In speaking about the future of his coming out, Ram shared his perception that coming out is a procession of point-in-time disclosures: "I became addicted to telling people . . . it becomes less, and less, uh, stimulating as you keep doing it. I'll probably get bored of coming out later on, but it hasn't happened yet." So, the linguistic use of the phrase "coming out" is broad simply because its definition varies depending on context. Consider the variation in the definition of coming out as seen in the following three sentences:

1. "I came out to my mom last month" (point-in-time),
2. "I began coming out after an epiphany I had on my eighteenth birthday" (coming out as a process), or
3. "Society encourages gay men and lesbians to come out" (could allude to either a point-in-time event or a process)

Although no participants spoke of coming out as purely a point-in-time event, as seen in Chapter 2, a few participants did ascribe a meaning to coming out that was based in telling one person (usually a parent). For example, Ari spoke of how most people knew her sexuality already. Therefore, for her, coming out means "telling the people who are closest to you"—for her this meant telling her mother and father. Based on her response alone it would appear that coming out was purely a point-in-time event. But throughout the rest of her interview Ari still spoke of coming out more broadly, and she framed it as a phenomenon rooted in self-affirming her identity and then expressing it to others when necessary.

As a culture, we have come to view point-in-time disclosures as so important that they oftentimes consume the minds of LGBQ youth. How will I tell mom? What will my friends think? These sorts of questions often lie at the center of internal struggles concerning the affirmation of an LGBQ identity. But the importance we place on situational disclosures leads to the perception that coming out is an entirely external phenomenon. It also contributes to the rhetoric that coming out has a definitive end—and that perceived "end" is the moment we tell whomever we define as "important" (parents, siblings, peers, a potential partner). But where do people get the idea that point-in-time disclosures are synonymous with coming out?

A few participants elaborated on how and why we view "telling" as central to coming out. Lee emphasized the role of common storylines and social stereotypes in forming our views of coming out. He emphasized that coming out is "not that one moment where you're at a family dinner where your whole extended family is over for Christmas and you're carving into a turkey and you clang your glass . . ." Such a stereotypical type of point-in-time coming out moment was mentioned throughout various interviews. Lee offered a bit more insight into where such perceptions of coming out are derived and why they are so pervasive.

> It's just like you watch these videos or you watch these shows . . . of course, you start watching the shows with, like, the gay protagonist—you watch their storyline. Of course, the breaking point is like "oh, when is he going to come out to his family" and it's this big thing and it's glamorized and this and that. But, when it comes down to it, life isn't a TV show.

Lee's recognition of common storylines and media portrayals of coming out brings up an important trait in our perception of what coming out means. Nobody lives in a vacuum. We all develop expectations and a basic understanding of social phenomena from outside sources, and these expectations are often drastically different from the realities of our own social spheres.

Most participants did not offer any details on where they derived their broader understanding of what coming out should be like. We all judge our own experiences against some sort of measuring stick. Lee and one other participant, Richard, view high publicity coming out stories in the media as the measuring stick against which LGBQ youth judge their own coming out. As Lee referenced, social media and pop culture likely have a lot to do with why we tend to view telling as being synonymous with coming out. From the coming out of Ellen DeGeneres' character on the 1997 sitcom *Ellen* to the recent YouTube phenomena of Dan Savage's *It Gets Better*, people come in contact with various interpretations of what coming out is, and what it means. The challenge then is for individuals to learn what is important to themselves and their own sexual identity formation and maintenance versus what they are being told *should* be important.

Richard, a 24 year-old gay male, highlighted just how much popular media and common storylines can influence our conception and expectations of coming out. Richard explained: "I wanted to come out in high school, I guess, in this classic television sense." He explicitly remembers watching the two-episode event of *Ellen* where she comes out to her close friends. He recalls how her identity disclosure was such a big deal both on the show and in the media and how her friends on the show were so surprised by the character's admittance that she was gay. This, and other media influences (such as *Degrassi*) gave Richard the perception that coming out means one or perhaps a series of monumental occasions dealing with outward disclosure (i.e., telling). He has since altered his vision of what coming out means to emphasize both self-affirmation and the sharing of his sexuality with his family and close friends.

Until recently, few television shows or movies have given viewers insight into the internal struggles that accompany coming out. Most often, coming out is shown from the perception of the privileged—that is, the storyline typically revolves around other people's reactions to the news. Recent shows like Fox's *Glee* are beginning to inform young television viewers that there is much more to coming out than simply telling someone. Media depictions of coming out will likely remain a primary source of knowledge for young persons exploring their sexuality, but perhaps with the proliferation of more well-rounded LGBQ characters in TV and film contemporary youth will gain a more comprehensive understanding of coming out as a gradual process which is internal as well as external.

Despite the prevalence of "telling" in popular media, most participants demonstrated a belief that coming out was about much more than simply disclosing their sexuality to a few other people. It was fairly common among participants to discuss coming out in the context of both a point-in-time event and a gradual process. Veronica, a 20 year-old who identifies as a lesbian, epitomized coming out as both a point-in-time event and a process. On her own volition, she took the liberty of highlighting the different uses of the term "coming out":

> I guess "out" in general would be "openly gay." Coming out to someone—it may not mean you're coming out to the rest of the world, but coming out to that person is telling them you're gay. I guess it depends on the context. *So, there's a situational coming out and there's coming out as a whole* (emphasis added).

This split between the situational coming out and coming out as a whole was similarly stated by Nathan, a 21 year-old gay male:

> I guess I view [coming out] as two different interpretations. There is the one where it's just kind of like people asking me if I'm gay and I will go "yes, I am." That's one form of coming out. Then there is the

more philosophical—that kind of delves into "what is my coming out story?"

For every participant in this study, coming out means more than *just* coming out in a single circumstance. In other words, those who referenced coming out as a point-in-time event typically talked about either a series of point-in-time moments that collectively comprised coming out or they discussed coming out as a gradual process. Participants such as Renee, Rachel, Gabrielle, Kelly, and Eden all utilized the retrospective phrase "when I first came out," which showcases the recognition of both a point-in-time event and the beginning of a career trajectory (if participants were speaking purely of a point-in-time event they would not say "when I *first* came out"—they would just speak of "when I came out"). Gabrielle, who talked about the temporal elements of coming out at great length, encapsulated how coming out is not a singular event. Rather, coming out is comprised of a series of point-in-time events, like a gradual process with many individual stops along the way.

> I think, as a gay person, there's always multiple coming outs. I mean, every person I meet on the fucking street, you know, if they realize I'm gay [they're like] "You're gay?"—"Yeah, I'm gay,"—once again, that's another coming out.

When Gabrielle spoke of "multiple coming outs," she was referring not just to telling multiple people—she was speaking of coming out multiple times to the same people, even oneself. Based on literature on coming out, one might assume that sexual identities are static, fixed entities. But, sexual identities are becoming increasingly fluid, and individuals are reporting having experienced a great deal of fluidity. Some people experience only an internal sense of fluidity as they move through a series of self-affirmations, and eventually come out externally only after they feel settled on a particular, terminal identity. Other people demonstrate fluidity by moving through multiple identities, both privately and publicly, each of which results in the disclosure of their sexuality to whomever they decide to share this information. This latter group often finds themselves coming out multiple times to some of the same people, even themselves. Consider Gabrielle's admission:

> I came out as bi-curious, and then I came out as bisexual . . . It took a lot . . . It probably took me like two or three years to really feel comfortable with myself saying "I am Gabby and I am a lesbian," and now I am, you know, so I think it was definitely a process.

This pattern of coming out multiple times to the same people was expressed by many participants. While speaking of the duration of coming out, most participants were referring exclusively to the outward elements of coming out—coming out to others. But Gabrielle's quote is particularly telling in that she brought into sharp contrast that coming out to oneself is also something which may include a series of point-in-time *self*-admissions or affirmations.

More than half of the participants in this study volunteered that they came out multiple times to themselves as well as to other people. One sexual identity may have remained for a period of months, only to be replaced by a new identity, and so on. The general opinion in many circles is that youth often experience a phase of questioning or bi-curiosity, but soon thereafter form a more concrete sense of their sexuality as gay, lesbian, bisexual, or perhaps heterosexual. Evidence from this study indicates that identity formation may include many more stops along the way. Despite the fact that identity formation can have many points of demarcation, coming out remains relevant throughout. There was no sense among younger participants that they should maintain a solidified identity for any particular period of time before engaging in self-affirmation or the disclosure of their sexuality. Participants recall feeling, at each of the points-in-time, that they had already realized their "true" sexuality, so there was no holdup in terms of affirming or sharing their sexuality with others. There is a common sentiment now—in looking back on the development of their sexuality—that each juncture in their sexual trajectory was a necessary change which served its purpose in helping guide them to their current sexuality (which we cannot assume is their final sexual identity).

Coming out multiple times to other people and even oneself demonstrates a solid indication of coming out as a career. There exists a clear difference between older and younger participants in terms of who engaged in coming out multiple times with different identities. Among my sample, the birth year of 1988 seemed to serve as the time of distinction. Participants born after 1988 were the group who cited coming out after each identity (or affinity) they self-affirmed. Recall from Chapter 4 that Ari demonstrated this interaction well. Ari (as well as many other young women in the study) came out initially with an affinity (i.e., "liking girls"), then as bisexual, and finally as a lesbian. These various self-affirmed identities resulted in multiple "outings" to many of the same people. Research has demonstrated that sexual fluidity is rather common among young women (Diamond 2004), but my data indicates that sexual fluidity occurs among young men as well. The cut-date of 1988 is based upon the data supplied by the 30 participants in this study, and it should not be seen as universal. However, the distinction is clear. Individuals in the older cohort initiated coming out only after their identities were fixed for a substantial period of time, while those in the younger cohort were more apt to come out multiple times as they moved through a series of sexual identities.

Although nobody in the current study suggested that coming out was purely a single point-in-time event, many participants refrained from speaking at all about coming out as a point-in-time event. Such participants choose instead to discuss coming out only in the context of it being a gradual process. One such person was Renee. For her, coming out is a gradual "process of [disclosing her sexuality to] friends and coworkers, and then family." Renee, like Gabrielle, recognized that the introduction of new friends and coworkers would equate to an enduring quality where the process becomes unending—that is, coming out results in a career.

Coming out as a Career

Participants frequently spoke of coming out as a process, but rarely did anyone indicate a clear end in sight. Consider Gabrielle's earlier admission that "every person I meet on the fucking street, you know, if they realize I'm gay [they're like] 'You're gay?'—'Yeah, I'm gay,'— once again, that's another coming out." Gabrielle did not specify an end to her coming out—in fact, her reference above to "every person I meet" signifies a career perspective of coming out. The sense that coming out could potentially be "re-engaged" anytime someone else questions or draws attention to an individual's sexuality upholds that coming out is not a process to be completed. Coming out is a matter of career management, not unlike other permanent elements of our lives. Individuals need not disclose their LGBQ identities in order to be engaged in coming out either. The management of one's identity— deciding when to speak of it, when to affirm, when to deflect, when to compartmentalize—is central to coming out.

The two themes of *coming out as a gradual process* and *coming out as a career* are similar in that they both recognize coming out as an ongoing progression. However, there is a sharp distinction between these two conceptions of coming out: a process is eventually completed, while a career is not completed, per se—it is merely managed. Recall from Chapter 2 that all participants spoke of coming out as a transformative venture. For some people that venture that was more of a personal journey centered on self-affirmation, while for others it was about the sharing of their sexuality with others (and oftentimes a combination of these two characteristics). It is this two-sidedness of coming out (i.e., internal and external) which resonates with sociological literature on *careers*. Careers are about the personal and social maintenance of one's identity.

The uniqueness of the career perspective of coming out is the notion that coming out has no definitive completion. It is a recognition that, as long as sexual minorities are "othered" in society, members of the LGBQ community will continuously have to engage in coming out. People enter and part from our lives continuously and our social spheres change, thus coming out endures. Athena, a 44 year-old who identifies as a lesbian highlighted this enduring quality of coming out: "You're always kind of coming out. Every time you're in a new situation where you need to mention who you are, you're coming out again." Such a perception means coming out is comprised of limitless ebbs and flows. For example, an individual may affirm a gay identity, share her sexuality with those who matter most, and come out at work only to be relocated to another city by her employer. The woman will encounter new coworkers and likely establish a new network of friends, after which she will face similar decisions of whether or not to come out to others.

There is a sense of both progression and regression that can be seen in careers. Erving Goffman (1959) originally spoke of careers in reference to the stigmatized identities of mental health patients. However, the term has since been used to refer more broadly to any permanent social strand in one's life course.

> One value of the concept of career is its two-sidedness. One side is linked to internal matters held dearly and closely, such as image of self and felt identity; the other side concerns official position, jural relations, and style of life, and is part of a publicly accessible institutional complex. The concept of career, then, allows one to move back and forth between the self and its significant society, without having overly to rely for data upon what the person says he thinks he imagines himself to be (Goffman 1959:125).

Goffman references there being both an internal and external element to the concept of the career. This important aspect of the career was seen clearly throughout my interviews with the participants in this study. Participants spoke frequently about coming out to oneself (internal) and coming out to others (external), thus bolstering the assertion that coming out is a career in much the same sense that Goffman asserted over a half century ago. Some participants did focus more on either the internal or the external elements of their career in discussing the meaning they attribute to coming out. Nevertheless, nearly all participants at least made mention of internal and external aspects to their coming out, thus supporting the claim that coming out is truly a career.

Careers are not completed; rather, there is a sense of continuity in the proceedings. Just as Gabrielle admonished above, Adam emphasized that coming out "is more of a continual effort just because, like I said before, any time you meet someone new you have to go through that process again." Individuals may come out to everyone in their social networks only to meet new people and find that they have essentially taken a few steps back in terms of their *degree of outness*. I am speaking under the assumption that individuals are interested and willing to share their sexuality with other people. But this assumption is not unfounded. The participants in this study who spoke of coming out as a career were also the same people who were interested in engaging in the broad disclosure of their sexual identity. For example, Renee, who speaks often of the career trajectory of coming out, feels that "when you come out it should be out to everyone." It makes sense that there would be a connection between the belief that coming out is a matter of full disclosure and the recognition that coming out is a career. If individuals maintain that coming out means disclosing of their sexuality to any and every one, it goes without saying that, for them, coming out has no definitive end in sight.

Outside of interactions with people to whom an individual may purposively come out, LGBQ persons also encounter numerous situations in which casual friends, peers, or even strangers question their sexuality or make a remark that beckons an admission of sexual difference. Some participants spoke of using humor or quiet complacency to avoid speaking to acquaintances about matters related to sexuality, but the awareness of such techniques reiterates the existence of career management. Brandon's quote from the beginning of the chapter hits on this very aspect of coming out: "It's a constant process. It's something that people ask you 'oh, do you have a girlfriend?' or something like that. It's a constant process, it's not something that you do and you finish, it's something you do for life." As my interview with Brandon continued he went into great detail about his perception that coming out is an unending endeavor:

> I'd say that [coming out] is a 3-step process: 1) the coming out within and having that self-realization of your sexuality, 2) close friends and family, and those that you know and work with on a daily basis, and 3) um, the disclosing of your identity where the topic just happens to specifically come up or you're specifically asked by a stranger or someone you just met or something along those lines.

Throughout the interviews, numerous participants spoke of parts one and two of Brandon's view on coming out. Of import here is his recognition that how coming out is never truly completed (part 3 of his definition). Public disclosure is always looming about, and therefore always has the potential to affect social interaction. Juxtaposing Brandon's step one with steps two and three, we also see a clear example of the internal/external two-sidedness Goffman described as being central to the career model.

In her telling work "My Revolving Closet Door," Suzanne Johnson (2008) speaks of the unending elements of coming out that continue to affect her professional life. As did many of the participants in the current study, Johnson describes herself as being very "out." As she explained, "At this point, let me say, I do not live in the closet. I am as 'out' at work as one could possibly be." Despite being very open and forthright about her being gay, each semester she encounters new students who are unaware of her sexuality. They oftentimes do not ask about the details of her sexuality directly—after all, people often assume others to be heterosexual until they unearth evidence to the contrary. As a result, sexual difference often rears its head in seemingly normal social exchanges. Johnson describes,

> I may be explaining to a student that I cannot schedule an advising session at 9:30 at night because I need to be home with my children, and the response will be a knowing smile. "Oh, your husband can't handle it by himself, huh?"

Moments such as the one described by Johnson call upon LGBQ individuals to engage in coming out. Even if she were to ignore the comment and navigate her way around the heteronormative assumption of her pupil, she is engaging in the career management of her sexuality nonetheless. Despite living in an affirming environment, having tons of social support, and being relatively out at work, she still has to evaluate her environment on a regular basis and respond accordingly. Such is the career of coming out.

So far we have spoken mostly of coming out as a career based solely on the external parts of identity maintenance. But as evidenced by participants like Ari, Ruby, Kelly, and Kyle, even the internal portion of the career may reemerge, particularly if one's sexuality remains somewhat fluid or changes across time. Each of the aforementioned individuals came out initially with one sexual identity, and then affirmed one or more different identities thereafter. This trajectory of affirming new identities holds true for 15 of the 30 participants in this study, indicating that the career of coming out is as internal as it is external. LGBQ persons who self-affirm a new sexual identity often find themselves engaging in a new wave of disclosing their sexuality to family, friends, etc. (as evidenced in the discussing of "multiple coming outs" above).

As is the case with all careers, as one gains experience, one's career becomes more manageable. At the very least, broad public interactions involving sexuality become more routine—that is, they become rooted in a somewhat formulaic, storytold testimony. Adam seemingly picks up where Brandon left off in his discussion of having to disclose his sexuality to whomever he meets. Adam explains the relative easiness of coming out that is prompted by gaining more experience doing so with more and more people:

> But, at the same time, it gets easier to the point that it's a non-issue anymore. Where the initial impetus of coming out to my parents, my friends—that was tough. But, with every day, every new person I meet it gets a little bit easier, just because I've done it before and I know who I am and who I can depend on.

Adam points out a common feeling among people who are engaged in coming out—it gets easier as you gain more experience. "I think as the years go by it's going to be easier," is exactly how Gabrielle put it. But, the perception that it gets easier is not shared among all participants of this study.

Michelle, a 25 year-old, who identifies as a lesbian, recognizes the career element of coming out. More importantly, she sees her coming out as a career because "everywhere you go there is a new group of people, new cliques, new, you know, everything." To Michelle, coming out means "being able to function like anybody else would be in your daily activities whether it be work, school, you know, house, anything. You should be able to do whatever you want with whoever you want." Michelle has spent most of her adult life structurally prohibited from fully engaging in her coming out due to her employment with the U.S. military. She has been unable to merge the personal and professional spheres of her life. In essence, she has lived a bifurcated existence as it relates to her sexuality. As she puts it, "I'm always looking over my shoulder like 'oh, did I do something that looked gay? Or, do I look gay today? And, always trying to make sure I don't stand out." For Michelle, coming out is more than a career—it is a career within a career.

The recent decision on the part of the U.S. military, spearheaded by an initiative from the Office of the President, to no longer enforce Don't

Ask, Don't Tell will hopefully change Michelle's circumstances. In an ideal world, Michelle should not have to fear for maltreatment on the basis of her sexuality. However, culture lag typically results from social and political changes of this magnitude, so the pervading culture of privacy regarding sexuality may undermine the dissolution of Don't Ask, Don't Tell, at least for a while. Consider our nation's history with anti-miscegenation laws, and the rippling effects they had on public attitudes toward interracial marriage. The federal court decision of Loving v. Virginia—which declared anti-miscegenation laws unconstitutional—was decided in 1967. Yet, as recent as the year 2000 states such as Alabama and South Carolina still had the unconstitutional wording that forbade interracial marriage in their state constitutions. Policy decisions, such as the repealment of Don't Ask, Don't Tell do affect coming out, but their effects are not absolute. Coming out will continue to be a career for LGBQ military personnel—but perhaps it will become a career that allows for a unified sexual identity rather than the bifurcated existence Michelle has lived up to the time of our interview.

Recall that one of the central components of the career model is that coming out continues to play a role in people's lives. One particular participant, Lee, spoke of coming out as a career, but there is a caveat to his belief. Lee represents the only participant who clearly stated disagreement on the idea that there is no end in sight. Whereas everyone else who cited coming out as a career felt that you never fully complete a coming out process, he had the philosophical notion that there *is* an end to coming out.

> For me, I feel as if once you come out, like, once you're not afraid to let people know you're gay, or you're not going to be holding it back, then I feel like you already fully came out. I don't feel as if you can come out "again"; granted, I know that there's new people . . .

So, although Lee describes coming out as a career that must be managed in perpetuity, he feels that once you are no longer afraid to disclose your sexuality to other people you are effectively "out." This demonstrates the only example of a participant seeing coming out as both a career and something that can be completed. Still, he recognized that, fear or not, individuals must continue to navigate a heteronormative society and proceed to manage their sexual identity.

H.G., a 51 year-old male who identifies as queer, had an entirely different take on the career element of coming out: "If you ask when I came out I would probably tell you 'never.'" H.G. has, in fact, affirmed a queer identity and disclosed his sexuality to many people in his life: family, friends, colleagues. He is simply making light of his view that he cannot ever *fully* come out. That is, he cannot be entirely "out" so long as there is a social expectation that certain groups must disclose their sexuality. For all the reasons discussed throughout this book, he is aware that he will never feel that he has fully and truly come out.

Discussion and Conclusion

Coming out does not start and stop in a single moment. Nor does it contain a clear end in sight for those who maintain LGBQ identities. Coming out is about the self-affirmation of one's sexuality (internal) and, if desired, the disclosure of one's sexuality to others (external). This two-sided quality of coming out is reminiscent of other literature on careers and it establishes coming out as not only a common and socially important phenomenon, but also a central element in the lives of most LGBQ persons in the U.S. Even more than this, coming out is about managing an LGBQ identity in a heteronormative environment.

Most participants in the current study provided evidence of coming out as both unending and permanently influential. But a few participants (namely Brandon, Adam, Athena, Michelle, H.G., Jason, Gabrielle, and Lee) elaborated on this belief and provided substantial support for the assertion that coming out is a perpetual endeavor that must be managed. Much of their evidence supporting how coming out is a career was based around the admission that they were constantly being called upon to confirm their sexuality by new people they met. Even the most "out" people will find themselves in new environments, around new people. This was pointedly stated by Adam, whom I interviewed while he was an undergraduate at a regional university. Adam was concerned about how he would adapt to the less gay-friendly professional sphere that he would enter after graduating and leaving the university setting.

> I do know that once I get into the upper echelon of the working world, it's like, even now, I work for two gay lawyers so it's not even an issue there, but once I do step out of that big, gay bubble, I do anticipate to have that conversation a lot more, which would be a lot easier if they would just go ahead and pass ENDA (Employment Non-Discrimination Act).

Living in the State of Florida, which does not offer state employment protections on the basis of sexual orientation, Adam knew that he would have to engage in a greater degree of identity management once he graduated (as of July 2013, discrimination is prohibited on the basis of sexual orientation in only 21 U.S. states and D.C.) . The two-sidedness of coming out will likely gain new meaning as he faces the decision to compartmentalize his sexuality or risk losing a job in order to remain true to himself. His experiences serve as a clear demonstration of how identity management is central to the career of coming out.

Despite the finding in this study that coming out is a career, the common sentiment in society (and within much of academia) is that coming out is a process that can be accomplished or completed. Considering the strong understanding among the participants in this study that one must manage an LGBQ identity continuously across the life course, why has most of society grown accustomed to hearing about coming out as a process that does, in fact, have an end in sight? Perhaps we have bought into heterocentric propaganda in multiple social institutions that depicts coming out as a method of confessing difference and nothing more. Or perhaps it is our optimism that sexuality will gradually become less and less of a divisive social force and it will therefore cease to be a necessary strain in the lives of LGBQ persons.

7

The Future of Coming Out

Perhaps the biggest takeaway at the conclusion of this study is that coming out is still a relevant concept. Prominent sexuality scholars have discussed periodically over the past ten or so years that "the closet" and therefore "coming out" are relics of the past. Supporting their claims are the many Northern and Western European nations that have unequivocally more affirming environments than that which is experienced in the United States. Some scholars have attributed the relative lack of support for equality on the basis of sexuality (along with many other social characteristics) to the high levels of religiosity asserted by Americans when compared to our benchmark peers. One way or another, the fact remains: coming out is still central to the formation and maintenance of sexual identities in the U.S. The themes discussed throughout this volume provide strong support for this claim.

Many young people today are not growing up "in the closet," per se, but the maintenance of an LGBQ identity still requires individuals to engage in some form of coming out. Even those individuals who are grow up in ultra-affirming environments, or are "assumed gay" based on their gender presentation, still find themselves engaged in coming out—if nothing else, simply to confirm someone else's suspicions or clarify someone else's false (heteronormative) assumptions. Even in an environment devoid of any disclosure imperative, the self-affirmation of an LGBQ identity requires an individual to engage in the internal elements of coming out. As one of the participants in this study, Nathan, pointed out, coming out is oftentimes not even done verbally. People utilize their physical presentation and dress in order to communicate difference, and therefore come out. It does seem to be true that the dynamics of coming out are changing. Less often are youth engaging in storytold monumental interactions where they come out collectively to their entire families. Coming out occurs much more casually, and it is often handled situationally with singular friends, family members, or peers. Although it may be less about monumental moments, coming out is still an influential part of the life trajectory for many, if not most LGBQ persons. And coming out is more than a mere process—it is a career.

The current study involves an exploration of the meanings attributed to coming out as well as a grounded investigation of the experiences of those who engage in coming out as it relates to their sexual orientation. As my singular predetermined research question, the analysis of *meaning* was informed primarily by symbolic interactionism. The remaining major themes of this project were all induced via a grounded analysis of the data: 1) the queer apologetic and 2) the new dynamics of coming out, 3) gender (non)conformity and coming out, and 4) coming out as a career. This concluding chapter engages in a discussion of key findings, limitations of the overall study, and directions for future research in this area.

Key Findings

Coming out is an important element in the lives of LGBQ persons, and it is widely considered to be a crucial element in the development of a healthy sexual identity among members of the LGBQ community. It serves a multitude of functions, not the least of which is self-affirmation and the public disclosure of a same-sex affinity or an LGBQ identity. As this study demonstrates, coming out is not the same for everyone. Individuals have varied experiences with coming out, and this is evident in the different meanings participants attributed to coming out.

Everyone has unique lived experiences, and therefore different experiences that comprise coming out. A singular meaning of coming out cannot be derived without trivializing or outright ignoring the broad variation seen across the participants in this study. Every participant did agree on one thing: coming out is both transformative and ongoing. Some participants cited coming out as a very personal journey centered on matters of self-affirmation, while for others it was about the disclosure of their sexuality with others. One caveat to this apparent universality is that my sampling was aimed at recruiting people who are or have been engaged in coming out. For LGBQ persons who have not engaged in the outward elements of such an endeavor, the meaning of coming out might very well differ. Longitudinal research that follows a cohort of young people, many of which have yet to form a sexual identity, may provide the best insight into the roots of coming out.

Variety in the *meaning* of any concept presents a methodological concern for studying any social phenomenon. The issue at hand with studying coming out is that researchers almost exclusively conceptualize (or operationalize) coming out as an external endeavor. As evidenced in this study, some people conceive of and define coming out as being entirely about internal processes (i.e., coming out to oneself). Future research on coming out should take into account that coming out is, at the very least, an internal as well as external interaction. Failing to account for the internal side of coming out can lead to disparate findings, thus jeopardizing the validity of the study as a whole. At minimum, researchers should share their conceptualization of coming out with participants so that a common understanding can be established. Otherwise the disconnect between researchers' intent with and participants' understanding of a concept may invalidate findings.

Most people live under the impression that to be straight is to be "normal." Heteronormativity is everywhere—in our households, our schools, retail stores, TV, you name it. Anything that is capable of sending or relaying cultural messages, is involved in magnifying the impact of heteronormative social arrangements. The pervasiveness of heterosexuality therefore encourages many people who experience same-sex attractions to feel that they must somehow maintain at least a partial foothold on heterosexuality. Despite being attracted *only* to members of the same sex, ten participants in the current study came out initially as bisexual. This interaction, coined in this study as the *queer apologetic*, affects a large number of LGBQ persons. Of course, I cannot generalize from my limited sample found in this study. But based upon the reception of this theme at professional conferences and from academic journals, the queer apologetic has resonated as an anecdotally familiar concept that had, until the completion of this project, gone academically unspoken and unnamed. The queer apologetic is essentially a form of identity compromise whereby individuals disclose a bisexual identity that they feel will be palatable to their family, friends, or even themselves. This compromise is based on the rationale that bisexuality simultaneously satisfies 1) their personal attractions for only members of the same sex, and 2) society's expectation that they be attracted to members of the other sex.

Individuals who engaged in a queer apologetic came out as bisexual for the sake of their family and friends and/or because they were personally not ready to let go of social conventions. People who engage in queer apologetics are not so much apologizing for their sexuality itself—they are apologetic about the *situation caused by their coming out*. In other words, people engaged in queer apologetics are not saying "I'm sorry that I'm gay." Rather, they are saying "I'm sorry that my being gay has raised an issue that is difficult for other people to deal with." Those participants who believed that coming out with a bisexual identity would be more acceptable to their family and friends were surprised to find that this could not be further from the truth. Family members and friends immediately pushed these individuals to affirm a gay identity. So, rather than easing the process, the decision to come out initially as bisexual made for a much more difficult route to disclosing their internalized sexuality which eventually aligned with a gay or lesbian identity.

Other participants who engaged in queer apologetics did so on the basis of their own refusal to let go of social conventions. The influences of heteronormativity led these participants to struggle with the realization that they are attracted to members of the same sex and may, in fact, be gay. Rather than coming out as gay, they chose to come out as bisexual; thus allowing them to hold onto "normality." Participants who engaged in a queer apologetic rooted in pleasing family were only engaging in the *public* disclosure of a bisexual identity. But, participants whose queer apologetic was based in their personal refusal to let go of social conventions were also deluding *themselves* that they were still interested in members of the other sex. Put more succinctly, the first group engaged in an outward apologetic, while the second group engaged in both an inward and outward apologetic.

Society is already resistant to accepting bisexuality as a concrete identity, particularly for men. After all, bisexuality challenges the artificial binaries that society imposes on us all (Lucal 2008). The queer apologetic includes the use of bisexuality as a transitional identity, and this has an immediate impact on those individuals who earnestly identify as bisexual. The use of bisexuality *only* as a transitional identity reinforces the essentialist belief in two discrete sexualities—gay and straight. It perpetuates the common (mis)perception that bisexuality is only a phase and not a concrete sexual identity. Thus, queer apologetics contribute to the marginalization of bisexuality not only throughout broader society, but also within the LGBTQ community. People are becoming increasingly open to the existence of a variety of sexual identities, and this may lessen the perceived need for an individual to engage in a queer apologetic. However, individuals who are attracted only to members of the same sex may still choose to come out as bisexual (or some other identity that allows both same-sex and other-sex attractions). As long as power and privilege are held by the sexual majority, people may feel inclined to hold onto heterosexuality—at least to some degree.

The queer apologetic explains why people who are interested *only* in members of the same sex may choose to come out initially as bisexual.

However, these are not the only individuals engaging in apologetic behavior. A related phenomenon was observed among participants who currently identified as queer, pansexual, polysexual, or fluid. The general public understands very little about these newly emerging identities. So in an effort to simplify their "crazy, progressive" ideals (commonly based on more open views of gender and sexuality than the typical person), participants who affirmed one of these identities oftentimes opted to coming out publicly as bisexual, or perhaps even gay (at least situationally). Their decision to do so is based in the belief that their family and friends will not understand their true sexual identity. So, they simplify things in order to communicate their difference to others. The motivation for coming out with a modified identity is similar to those who engage in an external queer apologetic—to please their family/friends. In both cases it is not so much about locating and confirming a sexual identity. It is about expressing one's public, social identity, and finding a place to fit in and be accepted. The basic purpose of any "apologetic" is to minimize disapproval and disappointment over her true sexual identity by disclosing a public identity she feels will be more palatable to her family/friends or herself. Of all the remaining threads found in my data, perhaps the most empirically important (and the one with the greatest implications for future research) is the trend of people coming out first with affinity, not identity.

Rather than disclosing a concrete sexual identity, people frequently come out first as simply having an affinity for members of the same sex. This technique of coming out with affinity (not identity) allows the individual to keep the door open on the possibility of future relationships with members of the other sex. It is also typically perceived, among participants in this study, to be more palatable to other people. Evidence from the current study suggests that coming out with an affinity is not necessarily about "keeping the door open" on other-sex attractions. Affinities are a natural precursor to the affirmation of an LGBQ identity. Prior to identifying as gay, for example, most young girls simply recall having an affinity for another girl. When I speak of "coming out with affinity" rather than an identity, I am referring to people coming out to themselves and others as "liking girls/women" or "liking boys/men." For example, when Lee first came out to best friend he approached it like this: "'I need to tell you something,' and she's like 'oh, what is it.' And I was just like 'I like guys.'" Nine participants in this study spoke of coming out *first* with an affinity, and this was most common among participants who engaged in a queer apologetic. Coming out with affinity rather than identity was seen by many participants as the safest way to come out, especially when they have yet to form a concrete sexual identity. Similar to coming out as bi-curious or questioning, affinities communicate an interest or at least curiosity in members of the same sex, but they are also characterized by a degree of impermanence that is perceived to be less threatening to family and friends (as well as the person who affirms such a sexuality). Although it only came up in nine of my interviews, based on the similarity of participants' experiences, I expect that many more participants came out first with affinity as well.

Not everyone who came out with an affinity was engaging in a queer apologetic. A substantial number of participants demonstrated that they express their sexuality by coming out with affinity simply because they prefer not to attach a concrete identity or label to their sexuality. Participants such as Eden and Ruby have grown weary of having their sexualities typified and stereotyped in ways that undermine the development of a healthy sexual identity. Their decision to express affinities is as much an effort to steer clear of being "boxed" as well a way to affirm that they like who like for their own reasons. Affinities, when used in such a way, can be seen as a personal or political choice used to assert difference without subjecting oneself to a barrage of harmful suppositions that work to trivialize progressive identities as nothing more than a new label for a gay identity. Recall that most people in the U.S. view heterosexuals as "100% straight" and everyone else as the "collective gay" so to speak. As such, being open and honest about one's sexuality while refraining from being trivialized is quite central to why a number of participants disclose their sexuality via affinities.

The differentiation between sexual identity and sexual affinity also brings to light another issue: our current language is inadequate for describing people's lived experiences related to sexuality. People commonly refer to their sexuality by expressing one of a handful of sexual identity or sexual orientations. Both "sexual identity" and "sexual orientation" are concepts that are used to describe a somewhat fixed identity. Thus, neither term is adequate for discussing individuals' attractions toward other people without presupposing a degree of permanence or adherence to cultural norms regarding what it means to be LGBQ. Even for those who come to affirm an LGBQ identity, affinities for members of the same sex are often an initial step in the formation of said identity. Expressing sexual affinities, then, is a more accurate way to refer to attractions without speaking of identity. Data from the current study suggests that sexuality is surprisingly fluid for both men and women, so adopting the use of "affinity" as a common concept can be a consistent way to refer to attractions without implying an identity. Such a move would prove beneficial (both academically and socially).

Academically, adopting the concept of "affinity" would allow researchers to better investigate younger cohorts who appear to be increasingly likely to steer clear of attaching an identity to their sexuality. Among the participants in this study who came out first as "liking boys/girls," all nine indicated doing so at a young age, most notably in their teens. At the time that they came out as "liking girls/boys" these individuals likely would not have identified themselves as gay, lesbian, bisexual, etc. In fact, some of them indicated that they maintained heterosexual identities for quite some time after affirming an affinity for members of the same sex. Despite not affirming an LGBQ identity, this group is of import to any research directed at limiting negative outcomes or advancing social justice for the LGBTQ community. By focusing on affinity, we can work to learn more about populations of people who may otherwise be missed. The social benefits of promoting the use of affinity as a way to express one's sexuality are as stated above: individuals can explain their sexuality without feeling the need to meet the expectations of a prescribed sexual identity. Considering how insistent U.S. culture is on the use of prescribed labels I am sure this sounds a bit idealistic and somewhat unrealistic to some readers. Only through the encouragement of innovative discourse can we attempt to change current modes of language that work to undermine the establishment of equality on the basis of sexuality.

Among younger cohorts, individuals who do affirm a concrete sexual identity appear to be identifying with more open, progressive sexual identities such as pansexual, queer, and fluid. Queer, pansexual, polysexual, and fluid identities are gaining in popularity, particularly among teens and young adults. There is a growing awareness that "queer" is an increasingly common sexual identity—in part because of its broad definition. Queer, which essentially means "different," is utilized by people with firm same-sex attractions as well as people who do not see gender as a defining characteristic used to determine potential partners. Here in the South, queer is still a very polarizing word since many people think first of its use as a pejorative aimed at sexual minorities and men who challenge traditional notions of masculinity. Hopefully as more and more LGBQ persons profess a publicly queer identity we will continue to work on reverting "queer" back to its original meaning: *different.*

We know very little about coming out among people who identify as pansexual, polysexual or fluid, but research on bisexuality may provide a clue. We already know that people who identify as bisexual, when compared to those who identify as gay or lesbian, are less likely to come out to others). Those who disclose a bisexual identity face the reality that few people in the general population understand anything about bisexuality. As newly emerging sexual identities, pansexuality and fluidity are generally even less understood than bisexuality. The lack of public understanding over newly emerging identities may explain why the meaning of coming out among people who identify as pansexual, queer, or fluid, is more about internal processes of self-affirmation than anything else. As these sexualities continue to emerge, we will likely see the meaning of coming out change across time.

Gender presentation has an impact on coming out, but the influence of gender presentation on coming out varies from person to person. Gender presentation can be broken down into two basic groupings: gender conformity ("sex = gender"), and gender non-conformity ("sex ≠ gender"). Most people operate under the assumption that "sex = gender = sexuality." In other words, people typically believe that all males are masculine and attracted to women while all females are feminine and attracted to men. In our heteronormative society, to have one's gender questioned is to have one's sexuality questioned (Lucal 1999; Crawley et al. 2008). So, a woman whose femininity is called into question will quickly find that her sexuality is suspect as a result, and the same trend holds true for men. At the same time, those individuals whose gender is not called into question still face myriad challenges in the formation and maintenance of their sexual identity. Coming out therefore often differs based on whether our gender falls in line with traditional expectations or not.

Considering the social expectation that "sex = gender = sexuality," gender conformity can lighten the load for someone coming out broadly because acquaintances and peers may simply assume that the individual is straight. For the next person, gender conformity makes coming out more difficult because the individual has to make a more concerted effort to come out to others. Again, because other people assume that the person is straight based on her gender presentation. During coming out, gender conformity does seem to be more well-received by family members and friends. Family and friends sometimes have a harder time accepting gender non-conformity than they do an LGBQ identity. On this basis, males who present more feminine and females who present more masculine often face additional difficulties in coming out. However, gender non-conformity is sometimes intentionally utilized in order to communicate broadly to others that one is not heterosexual. This tactic is based on the assumption that gender non-conformity amounts to "assumed gayness."

The effects of gender presentation on coming out may have to do with the meaning an individual attributes to coming out. For those who see coming out as a matter of full disclosure—that is, telling any and every one—gender non-conformity may aid the cause. However, those individuals who see coming out as being more about disclosing their sexuality to close family and friends may find gender conformity to ease the difficulty. Nevertheless, gender presentation can and often does have an effect on coming out.

The effects of gender (non)conformity on coming out highlights the link between gender and sexuality. Thus, *doing gender* is intimately tied to *doing sexuality*. *Doing sexuality* is heavily reliant on the suppositions we make on the basis of a person's gender, which also draws upon a person's sex category. Those who appear to be female-bodied are expected to be feminine, and to be attracted to men, so future studies on "doing difference" (West and Fenstermaker 1995) should take into consideration the interconnectedness of how we do *both* gender and sexuality simultaneously. One form of doing difference casts a shadow over other forms of doing difference. Due to the cultural stereotypes of gay men as ultra-effeminate and lesbians as manly (both characterized as challenging conventional notions of doing gender), public perceptions of gay men and lesbians are often sensationalized and rooted in expectations based on sex category. This is an important point in terms of doing sexuality since we are held accountable to our body and our sex category (Messerschmidt 2009). Between the stereotypical public perceptions of LGBQ persons and the actual lived experiences of LGBQ persons, doing difference in terms of sexuality—that is *doing LGBQ*—is still a concept in its infancy.

Sexual identities are not fixed entities. Although some people forcibly assert that they are 100% gay, or 100% straight, some identity work has to take place in order for anyone to stake such a claim. The participants in this study demonstrated that sexual identity formation involves a great deal of change and evolution. Put more simply, sexual identity formation and maintenance, and therefore coming out, is a gradual, unending process (i.e., a career), and a messy one at that. Individuals shift affinities and identities internally before settling on a more permanent identity, and these identity shifts may also lead to multiple coming outs. Even when someone establishes and maintains a "fixed" identity, new life experiences can lead an individual to take a step back and reconsider the "rules" of one's identity. A great Hollywood example of this interaction can be seen in the Kevin Smith film *Chasing Amy*. The lead character in the film, Alyssa Jones, identifies as a lesbian, but her eventual affinity for a man makes her question her interest in only women. Although the film engages in little discussion of her present sexual identity, one telling scene demonstrates the jaw-dropping reaction of her network of lesbian friends to this revelation. Alyssa's newfound interest in a man leads other people, and consequently herself, to rethink her sexuality. The scene also highlights a parallel between coming out to gay peers as being potentially bisexual, and coming out to family and friends as anything other than heterosexual. In both settings, people's expectations are challenged. Participants in the current study spoke of similarly telling experiences after which they found themselves altering their sexual identities.

Coming out is not a singular event. It is a process, or rather a career, comprised of many point-in-time events. These singular events may include internal shifts in self-perception as well as the outward disclosure of one's sexual identity. Most of the time, participants discussed how their internal shifts in self-perception led to "multiple coming outs" or multiple disclosures to the same people. Most of the literature on coming out is written from the perspective that we are studying a singular identity. After all, much research in the social sciences is concerned with cross-sectional data—focusing only on "the now." But, sexual identities are becoming increasingly fluid, and this fluidity translates to the possibility of coming out multiple times to some of the same people.

Even coming out to oneself often includes a series of point-in-time realizations or admissions. Multiple participants spoke of hanging onto social conventions (heteronormativity) and how this translated into graduated identities—that is, slowly letting go of heteronormativity. Gabrielle moved, almost methodically, through a series of transitional affinities and identities. During her early development she lived under the assumption that she was heterosexual. As time progresses, she came out as 1) liking girls, 2) bi-curious, 3) bisexual, and then finally 4) a lesbian. At each of these points, Gabrielle not only self-affirmed the affinity or identity—she also came out to others as such. This trend of engaging in multiple coming outs was typical of many participants, particularly young women. Participants indicated that they came out at each stage of their identity development primarily because, at the time, they wholeheartedly believed their identity was fixed and final.

The new trajectory of coming out, which includes people coming out with affinities, coming out multiple times with new identities, and engaging more and more in the affirmation of newly emergent, progressive identities, resonates with the final major theme in this study: that coming out is a career. Participants spoke often of both internal and external matters related to coming out, which reiterates the two-sidedness of the career model. Coming out requires periodic introspection and it relies on the maintenance (or rather, management) of one's sexual identity across the life course. Most participants indicated that coming is a gradual, ongoing process, but they also indicated that there was no clear end in sight. The resulting synergy of these two characteristics of coming out equates to a simple, but heavily understated reality—that coming out is a career.

Future Directions

By no means is the material in this book exhaustive of the informative and influential ways in which identity formation and maintenance affects people in contemporary society. Aside from the themes covered in this monograph, a number of other themes and trends emerged from this data that are deserving of sociological inquiry. One of the more telling trends was the tendency of participants to apologize for not having what they considered to be an "interesting coming out story." Some of the participants indicated at the onset of the interview that their coming out was uneventful and uninteresting, and that they were sorry for not providing me with (what they perceived to be) meaningful insight on coming out. Participants even went so far as to apologize for me having taken time out of my day to hear about their mundane experiences. Such interactions speak to the power of cultural influences on shaping our perceptions of coming out. As a few participants highlighted, much of what we believe about what coming out should look like is based upon broad storylines as well as Hollywood portrayals of coming out.

Richard emphasized the influence of popular media and common storylines in forming a belief that coming out should be an exciting, jaw-dropping affair. Richard explained: "I wanted to come out in high school, I guess, in this classic television sense." He explicitly remembers watching the two-episode event of *Ellen* where she comes out to her close friends. He recalls how her identity disclosure was such a big deal both on the show and in the media and how her friends were so surprised. Based on the portrayal of coming out on *Ellen*, as well as other shows like *Degrassi*, Richard expected an equally profound moment—a moment based in disclosing his gay identity.

> I was like, ok, I need to come out to someone, and I had a group of, like, my really, really close friends who I've known since I was born, so I felt comfortable with them over anyone. So, I came out to them one evening, and they really just didn't care, they were just like "ok." I

remember being shocked. I was like "no, I want you to be like 'whoa, oh my god,'" and they were just like, "ok, whatever." So, I remember being kind of disappointed in that.

Popular media informed Richard to expect surprise from his friends, so their mundane reactions disappointed him following his coming out. This, and other media influences gave Richard the perception that coming out means one or perhaps a series of monumental occasions dealing with outward disclosure. Richard was not alone in the perception that his coming out was dull or mundane. Brandon felt very much the same. In response to my question about what his coming out has been like he stated, very matter-of-factly "I would say very dull. It's very much . . . I guess, family wise, very inconsequential overall." As the interview progressed it became clear to me that his experiences were far from dull, but somewhere along the line he decided that it should have been more—more eventful, more tragic, more something. We often hear glorified stories of significant coming out moments and horrific stories of parental rejection and alienation. These sorts of stories may lead LGBQ persons to perceive of their own coming out experiences as mundane and boring. Participants also seemed to act as if their mundane experiences were the exception rather than the rule. Such perceptions likely have a major impact on help-seeking behaviors, coming out, and overall self-perception.

Some scholars contend that there is a disclosure imperative placed upon LGBQ persons (McLean 2007). That is, society imposes an expectation that LGBQ persons must come out and publicly acknowledge their difference. Public disclosure related to coming out is based in heterocentric ideology that expects people to confess and explain difference. It seems plausible that LGBQ persons will be faced with a disclosure imperative so long as most people assume that sex, gender, and sexuality are fused in a single form (thus leaving no room for difference). Many of the participants in this study engaged in conversation about feeling expected to come out. Most participants felt a societal-level disclosure imperative, while others spoke of a self-imposed imperative. However, not everyone felt an obligation to come out. Some participants felt that society simply prefers that LGBQ persons remain closeted, thus allowing society-at-large to ignore the needs of the LGBQ community. The perception of a disclosure imperative can substantially alter an individual's trajectory in terms of coming out. Further analysis of participants' views on the existence of a disclosure imperative would elucidate some of the external forces that complicate the maintenance of a non-heterosexual identity.

One of the more surprising findings in the current study was the lack of participants in my sample who identified as bisexual. As discussed in multiple chapters, various participants had identified as bisexual at some point in the past, but nobody identified as such at the time of their interview. One could question why I did not purposively seek out bisexual participants in order to obtain a sample that is more representative of the entire LGBQ population. I did set out to have a diverse sample in terms of self-identified sexuality. But I did not seek to include any specific sexual identities. I wished to avoid making the epistemological assumption that individuals' present identities are their final, authentic identities. After all, had I interviewed these same 30 people in 2008 rather than 2010, more than five of them would have identified as bisexual. Thus, a gay participant was interviewed as "someone who presently identifies as gay" as opposed to someone who has a final, "authentic" gay identity. That is not my assertion to make— sexual identities are influenced by the social, and supposed by the collective, but held solely by the individual. Asserting that someone's present identity is their final identity would fly in the face of a great many findings throughout this study. Even the nine participants who came out initially as bisexual, and later as gay (engaging in a queer apologetic), may not have final, authentic gay identities. The relative fluidity seen across many participants in this study reiterates that sexuality is dynamic, malleable, and far from finite.

The fact remains that bisexuality is still largely lacking legitimation in society at large. Participants in this study spoke openly about how bisexuality is marginalized in the LGBTQ community. They also conveyed their perception that many people who would have previously identified as bisexual now attach their sexuality to any number of more fluid identities. This last point begs the question: what is more influential—heteronormativity or dualistic thinking? It seems logical that heteronormativity (although based around an assumption of pervasive heterosexuality) would allow greater room for bisexuality than homosexuality since bisexuality includes (at least in part) other-sex attractions. But the family and friends of the participants in this study refused to accept bisexual identities based in their belief that they were not authentic (100% gay or 100% straight) identities. In fact, two of the participants, who presently identify as pansexual and "not identified," indicated having previously identified as bisexual themselves before choosing a more fluid identity. Their decision to maintain a more fluid identity now is based in 1) their desire to avoid being chastised by their LGBTQ peers, and 2) their recent recognition that bisexuality is rooted in a dualistic gender ideology with which they no longer ascribe.

Heteronormativity and dualistic thinking both greatly influence the formation and maintenance of LGBQ identities, but greater research is needed in order to discern their levels of influence.

Bisexuality is still very prevalent in the United States, so I found myself quite surprised that nobody in the current study presently identified as bisexual. Thinking back on conversations with a few of the participants, I could not help but wonder if more youth today who might have identified as bisexual a few years ago are choosing now to identify as pansexual, polysexual, or fluid. Or perhaps many people who privately identify with one of the progressive identities above show up as bisexual in quantitative studies on sexuality simply because they check the box for "bisexual" on a survey instrument. In reflecting on the recent surveys I have completed, of the available choices, bisexual is the option that most closely aligns with sexualities such as pansexual or fluid (which are often nowhere to be found on closed-item surveys). Future research on these identities could help explain these and other questions regarding the distinction between bisexuality and other emergent identities.

Much of the research on coming out is centered on investigating various factors that influence (encourage, discourage, or simply alter) coming out. These include family formation, religion, education, and peer networks, as well as many other social and demographic characteristics. Upon initiating this project I set out to avoid intentionally asking questions about any of these topics—figuring that such questions might incite artificial importance on these topics. By utilizing a more open set of questions about coming out, I aimed to see what factors would be discussed more naturally by each participant. My rationale is that if something truly impacts an individual's coming out then the individual will discuss it on her own volition. It may then be informative to investigate the prevalence and scope of influence for each of the following factors in my dataset: social support, family formation, fear of rejection, and characteristics of the individual coming out (age, race, class, sexual orientation, education, religion, and religiosity). Such an analysis would serve as a solid test of prior research on the real prevalence of factors that purportedly influence coming out since I did not directly ask for any of these themes. For example, race and social class were not the focus of my analyses in the current project. Similar to the findings in McCormack and Anderson's (2010) study of masculinity and homophobia, race and class simply did not appear to impact my participants to the degree that gender and sexuality did. Coming out is surely influenced by race and social class for some people, but those themes did not emerge as particularly salient in the interviews with these

30 participants. However, my next major study will revolve specifically around investigating the potential influence of race on coming out.

Moving forward, the single most important thing we can do is set our anecdotal knowledge or suppositions aside and continue to forge an open and grounded research program that enables us to unearth the uninvestigated, yet readily available, elements of social life. Future research on coming out should continue to focus on the entire career of coming out rather than how coming out relates to a person's present identity. Most of the interesting themes and trends that emerged in this study would have been missed had I relied on learning only about participants' present identities. As the popular adage goes "the journey is more important than the destination." It is not the identity itself, but rather the process of identifying, that informs us about social trends and symbolic meaning.

Appendix: Reflection and Notes on Methodology

As a researcher, I often find it helpful, if not essential, to go behind the scenes and learn more about anything that may have influenced a study. While reading a monograph I continually find myself thinking about three particular questions: Why did the researcher choose to engage in this line of research? What kinds of factors could have influenced data collection? What kinds of difficulties did the researcher come across while completing the study? In a few select cases, I have had my questions answered by a detailed Appendix in which the researcher covered these and other topics. I hope to provide the reader with a more comprehensive understanding of some of the issues I faced as well as some of the motivations I have for engaging in this line of research.

Reflection and Disclosure

Although I have worked diligently to remain true to the inductive foundation of grounded theory, I have remained honest in disclosing that I am bringing some theory and potential expectations to the table. Early foundations in grounded theory (Glaser and Strauss 1967) would emphasize the trouble associated with using any particular theoretical framework to guide my research. In my estimation, any study in which the researcher chooses the topic cannot rely entirely on inductive reasoning. Although I can appreciate the need in qualitative research for data to dictate the theory, I also believe it is natural and unavoidable that researchers incorporate their perspectives into the work. As is the case with many research studies, a series of seemingly unrelated events brought me to this course of study. It is helpful, if not necessary, that the reader understands my motivation for conducting this study.

Over the course of my academic career, which began back in the late 1990s, I have become increasingly interested in studying any and every thing related to the formation and maintenance of sexual identities. I spent my undergraduate years in a large public university with a very active social sphere. During these years, I found myself employed in a variety of leadership positions across campus, each of which was centered on welcoming and mentoring first-year students. These included serving as an orientation leader, an admissions counselor, a health and wellness peer-educator, and a resident assistant (RA) in on-campus housing. Each of these roles brought me in contact with young people going through the exhilarating, transformative, and oftentimes tumultuous life transition to becoming a college student. Needless to say, most college students refer to this transition as a liberating, life-altering process.

During my frequent interactions with first-year college students I had the opportunity to serve as the "parent away from home" for many students. I was typically anywhere from one to three years older than most of these students, but in a college environment the difference in exposure and maturity between a first-year student and junior or senior student can be quite large. Most of the meaningful conversations I had with students occurred during my tenure as an RA. Aside from helping students with homesickness or the general sharing of campus wisdom, one of the most frequent topics among both residents and other RAs was that of sexual orientation and sexual identity. Students would often discuss with me how liberating it was to speak about and share concerns about their sexuality with a trusted person or community. Until moving away to attend college, I had honestly never truly recognized the challenges and difficulties associated with internal and external processes related to identity management (the least of which is coming out). Further, I had not yet stopped to recognize that dominant cultural ideology in the U.S. was based around the social construction of heterosexuality as the only widely "acceptable" sexuality.

This is probably an opportune moment to share that I, myself, do not identify as having an LGBQ identity. This last admission is where I might lose a reader or colleague whose loyalties rest with a true standpoint perspective on conducting social science research. Among the many tenants of standpoint feminism is that women's and men's voices are truly unique (Smith 1987; Lorber 1994), and the same can be said of the voices of people with diverse sexualities. In terms of life experiences, I see great merit in this perspective. I could even take this statement one step further by agreeing with Collins (1990) that the relationship between two demographic characteristics (e.g., gender and sexuality) creates social categories that are unique in their perspectives and overall experiences. However, regardless of one's own gender, race, or in this case sexual orientation, I believe that sound sociological research can be conducted independent of the researcher's own characteristics. Even those who insist on research relative to one's own lived experiences will find it difficult to deny the importance of fostering research from multiple perspectives.

Now, let us return to the matter of my own sexuality. Although friends and colleagues may refer to me as "straight" I do not believe in placing myself unnaturally into the heterosexual portion of a sexual binary (Lucal 1999). My personal convictions place sexual orientation on much more of a continuum like the one suggested over a half-century ago by Alfred Kinsey (1948), and my political orientation is more in line with pansexuality. With that being said, I have always participated in sexual, affectual, and romantic relationships with members of the other sex and am therefore lumped by others into the neat little box entitled "heterosexual." Being associated with the most prevalent sexual identity, I rarely have to publicly or privately justify my sexuality or explain my affinity for members of the other sex. Perhaps as a result of my interest in studying sexuality and gender, even "progressive" colleagues of mine have been known to question me about my own sexuality. It could therefore be argued that I too have to come out from time to time, but in most environments coming out as heterosexual does not put me in a vulnerable position personally, socially, or professionally.

Although my interest and curiosity over matters related to sexuality began in my undergraduate years, they blossomed during my early professional career and my eventual return to college (i.e., graduate school) as I established and maintained more close relationships with students and colleagues who identified as LGBQ. As I completed my master's degree, I came to recognize trends in what my LGBQ friends and colleagues experienced in terms of affirming their own sexuality, learning to operate in a heteronormative society, and dealing with the public sharing of their sexual orientation. Anecdotally, I realized how coming out was much more than a purely personal undertaking. It was very much a social phenomenon involving internal processes along with outside influences ranging from family and friends to social institutions such as church and school to media outlets and the broader society as a whole. I also began to recognize coming out as less of a series of point-in-time events and more of a career in which individuals come out only to affirm new identities, meet new friends, change jobs, or relocate to another city and find themselves in a situation to potentially experience elements of coming out all over again.

My interest in sexuality, and coming out in particular, reached its pinnacle during the first year of my doctoral studies. It was during this time that I learned much of the methodological and theoretical foundations for empirically studying identity processes—particularly those related to sexuality. Also important to note is that, during this timeframe (the 2008 election cycle), the citizens of three U.S. states (including my home state) voted on and passed constitutional amendments limiting marriage to a woman and a man. This was a tough pill to swallow. Same-sex couples were being framed as undeserving of basic human rights guaranteed under the constitution, and much of this rhetoric was coupled with stereotypical caricatures of LGBQ persons. This political climate launched me into a research trajectory based around understanding broad cultural attitudes toward homosexuality. That line of research was conducted in an effort to better understand why people felt justified in limiting the rights of others on the basis of sexual orientation. My discontent with the rigid language and monolithic categorization used in many quantitative studies was one of the driving forces behind my decision to part from that line of research and engage instead in the current study using the methods discussed in this volume.

The remainder of my doctoral studies was geared heavily toward equipping me with the necessary methodological and theoretical tools to engage in my own scholarship concerning the state of sexual identities in the U.S. As a result, I am very familiar with and accustomed to speaking about the aforementioned areas of research. Prior to initiating my first interview, I had plenty of anecdotal and academic knowledge of the subject at hand. But it was exactly this knowledge that I wished to keep from affecting my research as much as possible—enter constructivist grounded theory (thank you Kathy Charmaz). In the end, it was my familiarity with prior research, coupled with my personal experience involving friends and colleagues, which guided me toward this field of inquiry. But once I embarked on gaining a grounded understanding of coming out, I abandoned all assumptions in pursuit of a set of data that was based entirely around the individuals whom I interviewed and their experiences with coming out.

The Climate Surrounding the Interviews

In any qualitative study there are things happening behind the scenes (socially, politically, situationally) which can influence data collection. I can say with confidence that the exchanges I had with the participants in this study were some of the most open, constructive, and engaging interactions I have ever had—personally or professionally. Feedback from participants confirms that the interviews were conducted in an open, affirming environment that encouraged individuals to share the very personal details of their coming out. Still, the social and political environment in the U.S. concerning sexualities is far from ideal. One of the major concerns expressed by participants was that of my intent and purpose with conducting this research. I learned this only though asking participants for feedback on their experience with the study following each interview. After completing a few interviews I made the decision to provide participants with a greater understanding of why I was engaged in this line of research. I explained that I maintain what Denzin (1992) calls a critical pedagogy. That is, my research places emphasis on progressive politics and social justice. This small tidbit of information was enough to dismiss any suspicions that I had an agenda with this study that could be perceived as harmful in any way. The interviews were conducted in 2010—a time in Florida when there was a lot of social research being used (and quite frankly misused) by opponents of marriage equality. This may have contributed participants' concern over whether my research could be used in a way that would harm the LGBTQ community.

Of all the questions that could have been asked of me, the most common was: "So what's *your* sexual orientation?" This simple question also sat at the center of the concerns discussed in the prior paragraph. I quickly learned that the only two people who queried me about the potential misuse of the study did so (at least in part) because they perceived of me as a "straight male." A few of the early participants in this study indicated at the end of their interviews that they were trying to "figure me out" during the course of the interview. I always concluded my interviews by asking if there was anything else participants would like to add or any questions they would like to ask of me. The most common questions involved learning about my sexuality. To some degree I anticipated this. After all, I had just concluded a 60-120 minute interaction based around the intimate details of their sexuality—it is only fair that I offer up a few details of my own sexuality in exchange. To be clear, I never spoke about myself during the course of the interviews themselves. Only after the completion of an interview would I speak of my own life in any way, shape, or form. I learned from these exchanges that there appeared to be no issues of reactivity involving my sexuality—quite simply because there was little to no congruity between participants' conceptions of my sexuality. Some participants had pegged me as a straight ally while others were convinced that I was gay (and everything else in between). Most participants indicated assuming I was anything but heterosexual purely because of my chosen research topic. There seems to be a general sentiment that heterosexuals surely would not be engaging in a research project based around LGBQ identities. The entire topic of my sexuality at least kept me sharply aware of the fact that reactivity is a constant concern in the conduct of social research.

Another major factor that bore influence on the interviews was the prevalence of two major social issues in the news: bullying and suicide. In September 22, 2010, Rutgers University student Tyler Clementi committed suicide after his roommate secretly streamed Clementi's intimate encounter with another man via webcam. Although Clementi's story garnered the greatest degree of media coverage, other stories of bullying and suicide were popping up in the evening news and on message boards at alarming rates. Consequently, the rash of suicides was occurring right in the middle of my data collection. The overall feelings of frustration and concern prompted by stories of bullying and suicide hung a cloud over many of the interviews. I recall one particular exchange with Gabrielle where she was answering a question about her experiences with coming out and she mentioned the influence of the recent stories in the media.

> I think in the beginning it was very bad because I wasn't confident in who I was, but now, I don't really give a shit and if you don't like me for who I am then you are not worth my time. And I think that sometimes it really does hurt to hear . . . we're on the 5th person who has committed suicide in the past three weeks and that's why I'm so big about activism.

She was not alone in being influenced by national news involving Clementi and other victims of bullying and suicide. Adam broke into a response about self-affirmation and learning to accept his sexuality where he spoke about attending a vigil just a few days prior to the interview. He pointedly shared: "My parents were at the vigil where I talked about how their actions nearly made *me* commit suicide." So the increased media coverage of suicide within the LGBTQ community definitely wore on the minds of multiple participants. But to what degree I honestly cannot say.

Other major stories that were in the news during the period of my data collection were the repealing of Don't Ask, Don't Tell, and charged dialog concerning relationship recognition and marriage equality. As with the media coverage of bullying and suicide, it was clear that these topics were on the minds of many participants. Less clear, however, is how they influenced the tone of the interviews and the overall disposition of the participants. Although I could not identify anything in particular (in the media, in the interview itself, or otherwise) that had a consistent impact on data collection I felt it was important nonetheless to speak briefly about these elements of the social and political climate of the time.

Limitations

Although this study adds substantively to the literature on coming out, it is not without limitations. One shortcoming is the overall lack of generalizability. As I stated early on, generalizability was never a concern or a goal, but it can be perceived as a limitation nonetheless. The experiences of the 30 participants in this study demonstrate some common themes and trends, but I have to be careful in making broad assertions based on my findings. The themes that comprise the chapters in this volume are resounding themes that were experienced by numerous participants. So, you might say that the scope of the sample was sufficient enough to enable me to draw some solid conclusions on matters related to coming out. The remaining limitations of this study are rooted in the limited sample size, sample characteristics, and the fact that participants are asked to recall past experiences.

My ultimate goal in obtaining a diverse sample of 30 participants was to allow for a more well-rounded depiction of the vast array of meanings people attach to coming out. Under ideal conditions, I would have preferred to have twice as many participants in this study. Such a substantial sample size would allow me to break my sample down by a variety of characteristics and therefore make some meaningful across group comparisons. For example, there is a dearth of literature on coming out among black and Latino populations. A larger sample size would have improved my ability to ascertain any racial or ethnic differences in coming out. Due to the nature of this study, and the focus on meaning, the ability to make many across group comparisons was not central to the study. But, it would have made for some interesting analyses nonetheless.

One of the biggest challenges with any qualitative study lies in obtaining a diverse sample. This difficulty is magnified when the study involves a "hidden" population such as sexual minorities. The most challenging characteristic upon which to draw diversity is what I call "degree of outness." LGBQ persons who *have* engaged in coming out are well represented in literature on coming out. However, few studies include samples of people who have *not* engaged in any outward elements of coming out. Relatively few of my participants have come out to only one or two people. The meaning and related experiences of coming out are likely very different amongst those who have are newly engaged in coming out. So, I have to recognize this as a limitation.

Most studies on coming out contain heavily homogenous samples that are white, highly educated, and of a high socioeconomic status (Griffith and Hebl 2002). I was aware of the lack of diversity in prior studies, so I set out to develop a better-rounded sample. In many respects I was successful in doing so. Among the 30 participants in my study there was a fair amount of diversity across most dimensions. However, the sample lacks any participants who identify as black and/or bisexual. The lack of anyone who identifies as black is a major limitation. Cultural influences and distinctive conceptualizations of femininity and masculinity would likely lead to some unique experiences of coming out among black populations. Bisexuality is central to my chapter on the queer apologetic, so it would have been great to have a few participants who currently identify as bisexual. Such participants would have provided the opportunity to observe how bisexuals are affected by the engagement of others in a queer apologetic. Also, my sample is heavily middle class, with only a couple of individuals located at either end of the class continuum. Then again, many Americans self-identify as middle class regardless of their relative income or education levels (Kelley and Evans 1995), so the predominance of middle class in my sample should not be surprising. Still, lower and working class individuals operate in environments that are generally less supportive of coming out (Appleby 2001), so the meaning of coming out might vary based on social class. But the current sample prohibits me from analyzing such differences.

A final limitation to the current study is the fact that, during my interviews, participants are asked to reflect on their past and recollect experiences related to coming out. The lens with which we view past experiences is affected by our current perspective on our social worlds. I have to acknowledge that participants' recollections are based in the process of recalling and then interpreting old information. For this very reason, some social scientists recommend not asking anyone to recall information that is more than six months old. Then again, I am asking people to recall experiences that have helped shape them in profound ways, and this is much different than asking people to recall more mundane experiences like the last time they visited a doctor's office (Wright and Marsden 2010). Although there are a few limitations to the current study, the findings and subsequent implications far outweigh the limitations. This study serves as solid evidence that coming out is still a relevant and influential concept related to identity formation and maintenance. Coming out is omnipresent and it affects even those LGBQ individuals who live in affirming environments.

References

Appleby, George Alan. 2001. "Ethnographic Study of gay and Bisexual Working-Class Men in the United States." *Journal of Gay & Lesbian Social Services* 12:51-62.

Ben-Ari, Adital. 1995. "The Discovery that an Offspring is Gay: Parents', Gay Men's, and Lesbians' Perspectives." *Journal of Homosexuality* 30: 89-112.

Benoit, William L. 1995. *Accounts, Excuses, and Apologies: A Theory of Image Restoration Strategies.* Albany: State University of New York Press.

Blashill, Aaron J. and Kimberly K. Powlishta. 2009. "Gay Stereotypes: The Use of Sexual Orientation as a Cut for Gender-related Attributes." *Sex Roles* 61: 783-793.

Bradford, Mary. 2004. "The Bisexual Experience." *Journal of Bisexuality* 4:7-23.

Brekhus, Wayne H. 2003. *Peacocks, Chameleons, Centaurs: Gay Suburbia and the Grammar of Social Identity.* Chicago: The University of Chicago Press.

Burleson, William E. 2005. *Bi America: Myths, Truths, and Struggles of an Invisible Population.* New York: Harrington Park Press.

Carpenter, Laura M. 2005. Virginity Lost: *An Intimate Portrait of First Sexual Experiences.* New York: New York University.

Carrion, Victor G. and James Lock. 1997. "The Coming Out Process: Developmental Stages for Sexual Minority Youth." *Clinical Child Psychology and Psychiatry* 2:369-377.

Cass, Vivienne C. 1979. "Homosexual Identity Formation: A theoretical model." *Journal of Homosexuality* 4:219-235.

Charmaz, Kathy. 2000. "Grounded Theory: Objectivist and Constructivist Methods." Pp. 509-535 in *Sage Handbook of Qualitative Research,* edited by N. K. Denzin, and Y. S. Lincoln. Thousand Oaks, CA: Sage Publications.

Charmaz, Kathy. 2006. *Constructing Grounded Theory: A Practical Guide through Qualitative Analysis.* London: Sage.

Chauncey, George. 1995. *Gay New York: Gender, Urban Culture, and the Making of the Gay Male World, 1890-1940.* New York: Basic Books.

Coleman, Eli 1982. "Developmental Stages of the Coming-Out Process." *American Behavioral Scientist* 25:469-482.

Collins, Patricia Hill. 1990. *Black Feminist Thought: Knowledge, Consciousness, and the Politics of Empowerment.* New York: Routledge.

Corsaro, William A. 1985. *Friendship and Peer Culture in the Early Years (Language and learning for human service professions)*. Norwood, N.J.: Ablex Pub. Corp.

Crawley, Sara. 2009. "When Coming Out is Redundant: On the Difficulties of Remaining Queer and a Theorist after Coming Out in the Classroom." *Feminism and Psychology* 19:210-215.

Crawley, Sara and K. L. Broad. 2004. "Be Your (Real Lesbian) Self." *Journal of Contemporary Ethnography* 33:39-71.

Crawley, Sara L., Lara J. Foley, and Constance L. Shehan. 2008. *Gendering Bodies*. Lanham: Rowman & Littlefield Publishers.

D'Emilio, John and Estelle B. Freedman. 2012. *Intimate Matters, A History of Sexuality in American, Third Edition*. Chicago: University of Chicago Press.

Denzin, Norman. 1992. *Symbolic Interactionism and Cultural Studies: The Politics of Interpretation*. Cambridge, MA:Blackwell.

Diamond, Lisa M. 2008. *Sexual Fluidity: Understanding Women's Love and Desire*. Cambridge, Mass: Harvard University Press.

Duggan, Lisa. 2002. "The New Homonormativity: The Sexual Politics of Neoliberalism." Pp. 175-194 in *Materializing Democracy: Toward a Revitalized Cultural Politics*, edited by R. Castronovo and D. D. Nelson. Durham, NC: Duke University Press.

Eliason, Mickey. 1996. "Sexual Identity and Bisexual Identities: The Struggle for Self-description in a Changing Sexual Landscape." Pp. 64-86 in *Queer Studies: A Lesbian, Gay, Bisexual, and Transgender Anthology*, edited by B. Beemyn and M. Eliason. New York: New York University Press.

Eliason, Michele J. and Robert Schope. 2007. "Shifting Sands or Solid Foundation? Lesbian, gay, bisexual, and transgender identity formation." in *The Health of Sexual Minorities*, edited by I. H. Meyer and M. E. Northridge. New York: Springer.

Fahs, Breanne. 2011. *Performing Sex: The Making and Unmaking of Women's Erotic Lives*. Albany, NY: SUNY Press.

Flowers, Paul and Katie Buston. 2001. "'I Was Terrified of Being Different': Exploring Gay Men's Accounts of Growing up in a Heterosexist Society." *Journal of Adolescence* 24:51-65.

Garfinkel, Harold. 1967. *Studies in Ethnomethodology*. Englewood Cliffs, NJ: Prentice-Hall.

Gates, Gary J. 2011. "How Many People are Lesbian, Gay, Bisexual, and Transgender?" *The Williams Institute, UCLA School of Law*. URL: http://williamsinstitute.law.ucla.edu/wp-content/uploads/Gates-How-Many-People-LGBT-Apr-2011.pdf Accessed on July 6, 2013.

Glaser, Barney G., and Anselm L. Strauss. 1967. *The Discovery of Grounded Theory: Strategies for Qualitative Research*. Chicago: Aldine Pub. Co.

Goffman, Erving. 1959. "The Moral Career of the Mental Patient." *Psychiatry* 22:123-142.

Goffman, Erving. 1971. *Relations in Public: Microstudies of the Public Order*. New York, NY: Basic Books.

Goffman, Erving. 1974. *Stigma: Notes on the Management of Spoiled Identity*. New York: J. Aronson.

Goode, Erich and Nachman Ben-Yehuda. 2009. *Moral Panics: The Social Construction of Deviance*. Chichester, U.K.: Wiley-Blackwell.

Gorman-Murray, Andrew. 2008. "Queering the family home: narratives from gay, lesbian and bisexual youth coming out in supportive homes in Australia." *Gender, Place and Culture* 15:31-44.

Grierson, Jeffrey and M.A. Smith. 2005. "In from the Outer: Generational Differences in Coming Out and Gay Identity Formation." *Journal of Homosexuality* 50:53-70.

Griffith, Kristin H. and Michelle R. Hebl. 2002. "The Disclosure Dilemma for Gay Men and Lesbians: 'Coming Out' at Work." *Journal of Applied Psychology* 87:1191-1199.

Grov, Christian, David S. Bimbi, Jose E. Nanin, and Jeffrey T. Parsons. 2006. "Race, Ethnicity, Gender, and Generational Factors Associated with the Coming-out Process among Gay, Lesbian, and Bisexual Individuals." *The Journal of Sex Research* 43:115-121.

Groves, Robert M. 2009. *Survey Methodology*. Hoboken, N.J.: Wiley.

Guittar, Nicholas A. 2013a. The Meaning of Coming Out: From Self-Affirmation to Full Disclosure. *Qualitative Sociology Review* 9: 168-187.

Guittar, Nicholas A. 2013b. The Queer Apologetic: Explaining the Use of Bisexuality as a Transitional Identity. *Journal of Bisexuality* 13: 166-190.

Herek, Gregory M. 1990. "The Context of Anti-Gay Violence: Notes on Cultural and Psychological Heterosexism." *Journal of Interpersonal Violence* 5:316:333.

Hutson, David J. 2010. Standing OUT/Fitting In: Identity, Appearance, and Authenticity in Gay and Lesbian Communities. *Symbolic Interaction 33*: 213-233.

Jackson, Stevi. 2006. "Gender, Sexuality, and Heterosexuality." *Feminist Theory* 7:105-121.

Jenkins, David A. 2008. "Changing Family Dynamics: A Sibling Comes Out." *Journal of GLBT Family Studies* 4:1-16.

Johnson, Olive Skene. 2007. *The Sexual Spectrum: Why We're All Different*. Berkeley, CA: Raincoast Books.

Johnson, Suzanne. 2008. "My Revolving Closet Door." *Journal of Lesbian Studies 12*: 59-67.

Johnston, Lon B. and David Jenkins. 2003. "Coming Out in Mid-Adulthood: Building a New Identity." *Journal of Gay & Lesbian Social Services* 16:19-42.

Jordan, Daren M. and Robert H. Deluty. 1998. "Coming Out for Lesbian Women: Its Relation to Anxiety, Positive Affectivity, Self-Esteem, and Social Support." *Journal of Homosexuality* 35:41-63.

Katz, Jonathan. 2007. *The Invention of Heterosexuality (with a new preface)*. Chicago: University of Chicago Press.

Kelley, Jonathan, and M. D. R. Evans. 1995. "Class and Class Conflict in Six Western Nations." *American Sociological Review* 60: 157–178.

Kimmel, Michael S., and Abby L. Ferber. 2010. *Privilege: A Reader*. Boulder, CO: Westview Press.

Kinsey, Alfred C., Wardell Baxter Pomeroy, and Clyde E. Martin. 1998. *Sexual Behavior in the Human Male*. Bloomington, IN: Indiana University Press.

Kitsuse, John I. 1980. "Coming Out All Over: Deviants and the Politics of Social Problems." *Social Problems* 28:1-13.

Krondorfer, Björn. 2007. "Who's Afraid of Gay Theology?: Men's Studies, Gay Scholars, and Heterosexual Silence." *Theology & Sexuality* 13: 257-274.

Lindley, Lisa L., Katrina M. Walsemann, and Jarvis W. Carter Jr. 2012. "The Association of Sexual Orientation Measures with Young Adults' Health-Related Outcomes." *American Journal of Public Health* 102: 1177-1185.

Lorber, Judith. 1994. *Paradoxes of Gender.* New Haven: Yale University Press.

Lucal, Betsy. 1999. "What It Means to Be Gendered Me." *Gender & Society* 13:781-797.

Lucal, Betsy. 2008. "Building Boxes and Policing Boundaries: (De)Constructing Intersexuality, Transgender, and Bisexuality." *Sociology Compass* 10:519-536.

Martin, Harold P. 1993. "The Coming-Out Process for Homosexuals." *Hospital and Community Psychiatry* 42:158-162.

Martin, Karin A. and Emily Kazyak. 2009. "Hetero-Romantic Love and Children's G-Rated Films." *Gender & Society* 23:315-336.

McCormack, Mark and Eric Anderson. 2010. "It's Just Not Acceptable Any More": The Erosion of Homophobia and the Softening of Masculinity at an English Sixth Form. *Sociology* 44: 843-859.

McLean, Kirsten. 2007. "Hiding in the Closet?: Bisexuals, Coming Out and the Disclosure Imperative." *Journal of Sociology* 43:151-166.

Merighi, Joseph R. and Marty D. Grimes. 2000. "Coming Out to Families in a Multicultural Context." *Families in Society* 81:32-41.

Messerschmidt, James W. 2009. "The Impact and Future of a Salient Sociological Concept." *Gender & Society* 23:85-88.

Miller, Andrea and Betsy Lucal. 2009. "The Pedagogy of (In)Visibility: Two Accounts of Teaching about Sex, Gender, and Sexuality." *Teaching Sociology* 37:257-268.

Messner, Michael A. 2007. "Becoming 100 Percent Straight." Pp. 361-366 in *Men's Lives*, 7th *ed.*, compiled by M. S. Kimmel and M. A. Messner. Boston, MA: Allyn and Bacon.

Ochs, Robyn. 1996. "Biphobia: It Goes More than Two Ways." Pp. 217-239. In *The Psychology and Politics of an Invisible Minority*, edited by Beth A. Firestein. Thousand Oaks, CA: Sage Publications.

Oswald, Ramona Faith. 1999. "Family and Friendship Relationships After Young Women Come Out as Bisexual or Lesbian." *Journal of Homosexuality* 38:65-83.

Pascoe, C. J. 2011. *Dude You're a Fag: Masculinity and Sexuality in High School (with a new preface).* Berkeley, CA: University of California Press.

Plummer, Kenneth. 1975. *Sexual Stigma: An Interactionist Account.* International Library of Sociology. London: Routledge and Kegan Paul.

Rich, Adrienne. 1980. "Compulsory Heterosexuality and Lesbian Existence." *Signs 5*: 631-660.

Rieger, Gerulf, Joan A. W. Linsenmeier, Lorenz Gygax, Steven Garcia, and J. Michael Bailey. 2010. "Dissecting 'Gaydar': Accuracy and the Role of Masculinity—Femininity." *Archives of Sexual Behavior 39*:124-140.

Rosario, Margaret, Eric W. Schrimshaw, Joyce Hunter, and Lisa Braun. 2006. "Sexual Identity Development among Lesbian, Gay, and Bisexual Youths: Consistency and Change Over Time." *Journal of Sex Research* 43: 46-54.

Rohrbaugh, Joanna B. 1979. "Femininity on the Line." *Psychology Today* 13:30-42.

Rust, Paula C. 1993. "'Coming Out' in the Age of Social Constructionism: Sexual Identity Formation among Lesbian and Bisexual Women." *Gender and Society* 7:50-77.

Rust, Paula C. 1995. *Bisexuality and the Challenge to Lesbian Politics: Sex, Loyalty, and Revolution*. New York: NYU Press.

Rust, Paula C. Rodríguez. 2000. *Bisexuality in the United States: A Social Science Reader*. New York: Columbia University Press.

Savin-Williams, Ritch C. 1989. "Coming Out to Parents and Self-esteem among Gay and Lesbian Youths." *Journal of Homosexuality* 18:1-35.

Savin-Williams, Ritch C. 1998. "The Disclosure to Families of Same-sex Attractions by Lesbian, Gay, and Bisexual Youths." *Journal of Research on Adolescence* 8: 49-68.

Savin-Williams, Ritch C. 2001. *Mom, Dad. I'm Gay. How Families Negotiate Coming Out*. Washington, DC: American Psychological Association.

Savin-Williams, Ritch C. and Eric M. Dube. 1998. "Parental Reactions to Their Child's Disclosure of a Gay/Lesbian Identity." *Family Relations* 47:7-13.

Schilt, Kristen, and Laurel Westbrook. 2009. "Doing Gender, Doing Heteronormativity: 'Gender Normals,' Transgender People and the Social Maintenance of Heterosexuality." *Gender & Society 23*:440–464.

Schlenker, Barry R. and Bruce W. Darby. 1981. "The Use of Apologies in Social Predicaments." *Social Psychology Quarterly* 44: 271-278.

Sears, James T. and Walter L. Williams. 1997. *Overcoming Heterosexism and Homophobia: Strategies that Work*. New York: Columbia University Press.

See, Helena and Ruth Hunt. 2011. "Bisexuality and Identity: The Double-edged Sword: Stonewall Research into Bisexual Experience." *Journal of Bisexuality* 11:290-299.

Seidman, Steven. 2002. *Out of the Closet?* New York: Routledge.

Seidman, Steven, Chet Meeks, and Francie Traschen. 1999. "Beyond the Closet? The Changing Social Meaning of Homosexuality in the United States." *Sexualities* 2:9-34.

Shallenberger, David. 1996. "Reclaiming the Spirit: the Journeys of Gay Men and Lesbian Women toward Integration." *Qualitative Sociology* 19:195-215.

Smith, Dorothy E. 1987. *The Everyday World as Problematic*. Boston, MA: Northeastern University Press.

Strauss, Anselm and Juliet Corbin. 1998. *Basics of Qualitative Research: Techniques and Procedures for Developing Grounded Theory*. Thousand Oaks, CA: Sage.

Teman, Eric D. 2011. "I Just Like Guys/Girls." *Qualitative Inquiry* 17:875.

Waldner, Lisa K. and Brian Magruder. 1999. "Coming Out to Parents." *Journal of Homosexuality* 37:83-100.

Weeks, Jeffrey. 2003 "Necessary Fictions: Sexual Identities and the Politics of Diversity." Pp. 122-131 in *Sexualities and Society: A Reader*, edited by J. Weeks, J. Holland, and M. Waites. Malden, MA: Blackwell.

Weinberg, Martin S., Colin J. Williams, and Douglas W. Pryor. 1994. *Dual Attraction: Understanding Bisexuality*. New York: Harrington Park Press.

West, Candace and Sarah Fenstermaker. 1995. "Doing Difference." *Gender and Society* 9:8-31.

West, Candace and Don H. Zimmerman. 1987. "Doing Gender." *Gender and Society* 1:125-151.

Wright, James D. and Peter V. Marsden. 2010. *Handbook of Survey Research.* Bingley, UK: Emerald.

Yep, Gust A. 2002. "From Homophobia and Heterosexism to Heteronormativity: Toward the Development of a Model of Queer Interventions in the University Classroom." *Journal of Lesbian Studies* 6:163-176.

Yon-Leau, Carmen and Miguel Munoz-Laboy. 2010. "'I Don't Like to Say that I'm Anything': Sexuality Politics and Cultural Critique among Sexual-minority Latino Youth." *Sexuality Research and Social Policy* 7:105-117.

Index

About the Book

Nicholas Guittar draws on deeply personal interviews with young people to enhance our understanding of "coming out," revealing the changing dynamics of sexual identity.

Guittar explores how mainstream norms continue to assert their influence over those with nonnormative sexualities. He also highlights the wide spectrum of coming out experiences. His important work sheds light on why, even though fewer people may remain closeted today than in the past, coming out is not a one-time event, but a lifetime process.

Nicholas A. Guittar is assistant professor of sociology at the University of South Carolina Lancaster.